REALIZING
the
PRESENCE
of the
SPIRIT

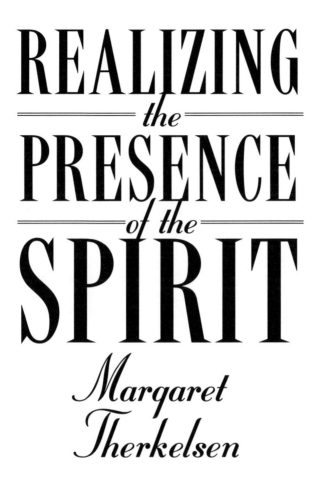

REALIZING *the* PRESENCE *of the* SPIRIT

Margaret Therkelsen

Fleming H. Revell
A Division of Baker Book House
Grand Rapids, Michigan 49516

© 1998 by Margaret Therkelsen

Published by Fleming H. Revell
a division of Baker Book House Company
P.O. Box 6287, Grand Rapids, MI 49516-6287

Printed in the United States of America

Library of Congress Cataloging-in-Publication Data

Therkelsen, Margaret, 1934–
    Realizing the presence of the Spirit / Margaret Therkelsen.
        p.   cm.
    Includes bibliographical references.
    ISBN 0-8007-5669-X (paper)
    1. Holy Spirit. 2. Presence of God. 3. Therkelsen, Margaret, 1934– . I. Title
BT123.T47   1998
231'.3—dc21   98-21490

Scripture quotations are from the King James Version of the Bible.

For current information about all releases from Baker Book House, visit our web site:
                http://www.bakerbooks.com

No words could express my eternal appreciation to my beloved husband of thirty-one years in typing the manuscript for this book.
My heartfelt gratitude to Duane and Bonnie Kinslow for typing the original study which led to this book.

Contents

Introduction

There is such a heart cry on the part of thousands of people today for a deeper, more satisfying relationship with God. They cry even as Job cried centuries ago, "Oh that I knew where I might find him! That I might come even to his seat" (Job 23:3). Verse 5 of the same chapter goes on to say, "I would know the words which he would answer me, and understand what he would say unto me."

Intimacy! Fulfillment! God himself would be our friend, and we would allow him more and more dominion and control of our lives, because we would know him better and better and trust him more and more.

How does this friendship with God unfold?

First, it can only unfold if we have asked Jesus into our hearts and believe he truly comes in. If he has been invited in, then his divine Holy Spirit *is within!* Our relationship with the Holy Spirit is unlike any other relationship, though it bears some resemblance to other relationships. It is different because we are visible and he is invisible, we are full of self-will and personality and he is gentle and soft-spoken, speaking in a still, small voice. We must learn to hear him speak in quietness and peace deep within our human spirit.

Second, he comes into our human spirit and takes up residency there, but we live so much from our soul realm—our emotions, mind, self-will, and personality—

that we are unaware of him so much of the time. Even as Christians we live out of our self-effort and self-sufficiency, not out of him, except occasionally.

Third, our soulish realm is so sinful and fallen, so bent in on itself, so self-aware and self-focused, we are pervaded with a stronger sense of "me" than "him." Unless we deliberately turn toward him daily, in separated times with him, and allow him opportunity to teach us how he reacts and responds to us, we are too full of ourselves even to know he is within. And our friendship cannot grow as he yearns for it to grow. Jesus said in John 15:15, "I call you friends." Verse 14, "You are my friends if you do whatever I demand of you."

Last, the friendship is based on our allowing the Holy Spirit to lovingly correct us, mold us, and conform us to be like Jesus. This means we are open to the life of the triune God in us taking over more and more so we decrease and he increases (John 3:30). Then we learn what God's commandments are and obey them, through the power of the Holy Spirit. Allowing the Holy Spirit any leverage over the power of our personality and will pleases God, and he honors any submission to him with a keener sense of his presence.

This is a how-to book; how to allow the Holy Spirit more access and freedom in us to help us. He will reveal our motives and intents (Heb. 4:12). He will convict lovingly our sin against him so we can see it and repent (John 16:8). He teaches us what we need to know (John 14:26). He confronts and loves us (1 John 4:16). We love him for pointing selflessly and quickly to Jesus Christ within us (John 16:7–15). As the Father draws us (John 6:44) to Jesus, the precious Holy Spirit helps us to come into the very presence of our wonderful Lord (John 14:16–27). Second Corinthians 3:17 says, "Now the Lord is that Spirit: and where the Spirit of the Lord is, there is liberty." In the mystery of the Trinity, Jesus is the Holy Spirit living within us during this dispensation of the Holy Spirit, yet Jesus Christ is at the right hand of God the Father, exalted and received of the Father, the promise of the Holy Ghost (Acts 2:32–33).

When we wait on God, the Holy Spirit is allowed time and access to be quickened within our human spirit, stirring in us the love of God (Rom. 5:5). The Holy Spirit, brings us into Jesus' presence. There will be many times as we linger in worship and adoration at Jesus' feet that we will sense the awe and wonder of the majestic God the Father drawing us closer to himself (Heb. 9:11–14; 10:19–23).

As we linger in the presence of the Triune God, each person of that Trinity becomes more pronounced. The waiting gives the Trinity admittance into our human life and spirit. What great mystery surrounds this, but because of the indwelling Holy Spirit, God's life is always available to us (Ephesians 1–2). By giving him opportunity through biblical patterns of waiting *on* him and *for* him and listening to his presence and voice within, we learn how to be a more intimate friend with Father, Son, and Holy Spirit.

It must be done his way, but his way truly is best. He wants to take us out of the ruts of self-love, self-preoccupation, and self-will, just to name a few, and move us into the high country of communion with him. He wants so to reveal himself to us that we fall deeply in love with him. He will more and more pour his love out on us and through us. Are you ready and willing to embark on life's greatest adventure? He waits eagerly and lovingly for you. "Christ dwells in us as a life in a life, inspiring us with His own temper and disposition. Our words and spiritual being, our power of willing and living and acting, within these He comes and dwells in us a divine, hidden, but mighty power and operation."[1]

The Father Draws Us

And therefore will the LORD wait, that he may be
gracious unto you, and therefore will he be exalted,
that he may have mercy upon you: for the LORD is a
God of judgment: blessed are all they that wait for
him.

Isaiah 30:18

The rains came in the night and cleared the sky
once again of cloudiness and pollution. The
morning was fresh and vital, symbolizing the
renewing power of God. As I awakened I felt
the irresistible drawing of the indwelling Holy Spirit to
come away with him to our secret place of exchange. I
threw back the covers and made my way down the hall
to my hiding place of prayer. As I went I reflected on the

wonder of his willingness to reveal himself to anyone who is available. During twenty-five years of daily fellowship a special relationship of love and friendship had grown and dramatically impacted my life. This relationship had become so captivating that I was eager to interact with him on this morning. I was aware of the richness of the dialogue that was awaiting me there. My heart was already responding, "Speak, Lord; your servant hears."

I began by sitting quietly but expectantly, opening my heart and giving the Holy Spirit control over this hour. In the next few minutes I entered into his love so completely that I forgot about time (Rom. 5:5). I heard his familiar voice say, "You are not my servant, but you are my beloved daughter."

That statement touched a place in me that only he can touch. I felt bathed in his love, as the earth must have felt by the rains that had come in the night. An overflowing realization caused me to discern his nearness. Such love flooded my heart that I was lifted, strengthened, and encouraged beyond what any words are able to convey. In those seemingly brief minutes of quiet, I was renewed and refreshed in our friendship.

"The words that I speak unto you, they are spirit, and they are life," Jesus says to us in John 6:63. Is it not unbelievable that we can experience the reality of this Scripture in our daily time of prayer? But this is what I had just experienced in my time with the Holy Spirit bringing me into the presence of Jesus. All the cloudiness of my heart was lifted. I *am* accepted in the Beloved, as Ephesians 1:6 says. His words to me were spirit yet so very life-giving. The uplift of his word to me remained for days, even as I continued to come to him daily. One must come daily to receive such a blessing. Even now the faithfulness of the Holy Spirit encourages me as I think about it. His indwelling presence speaks and acts from such unbelievable, unconditional love that it is able to renew and heal. Nothing we can experience today is more precious than his companionship!

If the indwelling Holy Spirit can and will speak to me, he can and will speak to anyone! The secret to experiencing this kind of relationship with God is time and being available to wait and listen expectantly. He has no special children or favorites; he longs for close, intimate companionship with every single child he has. If you are a believer that has invited him into your human spirit or heart, the miracle of all miracles is that he enters. Though we are broken, earthly vessels, so fragile, so wounded and broken by sin, he is truly the treasure of our lives, as 2 Corinthians 4:7 reminds us.

The place of residence of the human spirit within the body is not known. We just know there is a place created by God within this earthen vessel that he never leaves or forsakes after he enters. He comes in to stay, yearning to manifest his presence as fully as we will allow.

He wants us to live to the fullest extent with him there. What does this mean? We might first think about what it means to live to the fullest with others in the human realm. To live fully with others means we must communicate not only by speaking to them but also by listening to them. Then we will make the proper response so that our interaction at all levels will exhibit mutual trust. Most of all, we will forget about ourselves and see what we can learn from others. If these things are so in the flesh, why can we not apply them to our relationship with our heavenly Father?

The Holy Spirit takes our hand and leads us to this secret, hidden-away place within as we enter into prayer each day. The Holy Spirit is our link to the eternal realm. Prayer and the Scriptures open the door to his abiding place within so we can not only enter in periodically but also learn truly to remain with him there, as John chapter 15 reveals.

But maybe you are saying, "Margaret, what does it mean 'he is within us'? Can I really reach him somehow, some way, so we can talk together? Does he, the God of the universe, really want intimate companionship with me? How can it be?

"My personality and self-will are so strong and proud, is there real hope for me to learn how to allow him to be the dominant one? If he is inside of me somewhere, how in the world do I get in touch with a bodiless, invisible entity when I am so visible and aware of myself? How do I get quiet enough to hear him?

"What does the Bible say about this unusual relationship? Who is the Holy Spirit, and what is his basic role in the life of a believer? If he is so important, why have we not heard more about all this? How is it done? What is his part, what is my part?

"If all the Bible says is true, that we are to know his presence and his voice, what has gone wrong? What hinders his living in me so I am aware of him and moving in harmony with him?"

There are many answers, I am sure, to these significant questions, but I want to mention what I feel are the three basic reasons for our confusion about the indwelling Holy Spirit.

1. We do not know God's Word. We err and continue to do so because we do not know the Scriptures, as Jesus says in Matthew 22:29 and Mark 12:24, 27. God says the Israelites always erred in their hearts because they refused to obey his voice or word (Heb. 3:10; Exod. 20:18–20). Our main error is that we do not even know what the Bible says about the Holy Spirit, much less how to walk in obedience to what the Scripture says.

My husband, who is a hospital chaplain, knew a man who was told by his doctor that he had cancer and had only three months to live. He suddenly came alive to the fact that he had been way too casual in his obedience to the Word of God and was ignorant of what the Bible really teaches. He said, "I began to put into practice every word God had spoken to me through reading the Scriptures and the sermons that I had heard. I had never really lived out the Scriptures and taken them as the absolute Word of God Almighty. I began to trust and have faith in what God says in the Bible. I staked my whole life on it." This man, told by doctors that he had only months to live, now several years later is doing well.

We are so far from cherishing God's sacred Word. We are so far from believing that it is the final, binding Word of God. We fail to appropriate the empowerment of the indwelling Holy Spirit to live the truth of the Word within us and through us.

The most crucial pattern for getting in touch with Jesus within is found in the many Old and New Testament Scriptures dealing with waiting for God and on God and listening to know his beloved and divine voice through the indwelling Holy Spirit. Allowing him to well up within us and be present to us is allowing him to be alive within us.

Somehow, in an extremely pushed and busy world, a world of desperate need, we have taken more seriously the Scriptures on service and ministry to others. Ministry to others involves going and doing. We have nearly ignored the Scriptures that tell us, "Know ye not that your body is the temple of the Holy Ghost which is in you?" (1 Cor. 6:19). Knowing that he is within us involves waiting on him until he tells us what to do. He has a personality and is waiting to develop a relationship, a unique companionship, with you. When we run so much that we fail to sit and listen to his word to us, much less believe it, we are prohibiting his life from coming forth (Gal. 2:20).

Colossians 1:27 says, "Christ in you, the hope of glory." Jesus said, "The kingdom of God is within you" (Luke 17:21). When we ask Jesus into our heart, he comes and the Holy Spirit sheds abroad the love of God. Second Corinthians 3:17 reminds us, "Now the Lord is the Spirit and where the Spirit is, there is liberty." We need a growing awareness of him and all that he is. Since this is the case, the believer needs a growing sensitivity to friendship with him. That is Jesus revealed through the Holy Spirit. He is always available, accessible, and yearning to guide, instruct, and help us. He wants to teach us how to receive from him all we need. He is Savior and friend!

One further factor must be stated here. The Bible teaches an amazing thing about the Indwelling Presence. In John 14:23 Jesus says, "If a man loves me, he will keep my words: and my Father will love him, and *we* will come unto him, and make our abode with him" (emphasis added). We are promised a relationship not only with the Holy Spirit but also with Jesus and the Father. It is absolutely unbelievable, yet this relationship is plainly stated in this passage. I have come to believe this verse. I do not know what you believe, but I want to tell you that out of many rich experiences over the last few years, Jesus has revealed the Father to me in startling new ways, for which I praise him. Jesus says to Philip in John 14:9, "He that has seen me has seen the Father."

We invite Jesus into our hearts through the ministry of the Holy Spirit. As the Holy Spirit empowers us, we walk in obedience to Jesus' commandment to love even as he has loved us, and the Father takes up his abode in us! I truly believe we are to have an expanding consciousness of the Trinity throughout our lifelong pilgrimage here.

2. We do not know how to relate to the Holy Spirit. We have failed, except in certain sectors of the church universal, to teach Christian people how to relate and be a friend to the indwelling Holy Spirit. We have invited people to receive him, to be born again, but have failed often to teach them how to cultivate and deepen the relationship, even to apply basic guidelines for how human relationships are enriched to our relationship with him. I realize there is a dearth of relating skills in all of our lives because of the sins others have committed against us and sins we have committed, which build barriers to communication. Even if we have been taught to receive Jesus as Lord by allowing the Holy Spirit more control, we sometimes still have trouble allowing him to be who he is. We often have no role models for cultivating his ongoing life in us.

A short time ago I was sharing in a western community in a church which had a beautiful gothic structure— a church of obvious affluence but great spiritual need. At the lunch break on Saturday a man approached me, deeply offended by my assertion that not only does God long for intimacy with us, but we, enabled by the Holy Spirit, enter that friendship through times of prayer and Scripture reading.

"I don't know who you think you are, but I'll tell you who I am," he said. "I've been in this church all my life. My family started this community, and I never heard this kind of rubbish before in my life. I resent you saying that there are things I've missed in my relationship with God, and I refuse to stay and listen to this dribble. I find it totally offensive."

I was so stricken with compassion for this dear person and shocked over his response, I had to sit down before I fell down. Thank the Lord for the pew behind me.

"I am so deeply sorry that all this is so new to you," I said, "but God does want to be your dearest friend. Won't you sit down with me and maybe we could pray over this?"

"I am too angry to pray, and I have no need to talk with you about this anymore!" And with that he turned on his heel and was gone.

Tragically, this lack of teaching within the church on how to become more comfortable and close to God is not uncommon in some reaches of the church universal today. May I say there has been a lot of prayer not only for this man but also for others like him?

3. We like to be in control. We tend to operate almost solely out of fleshly, ego-centered power. Our strong self-will and self-bias, our self-assertiveness and self-sufficiency, are in control rather than allowing the Holy Spirit to do what he wants to do, in his way and in his power (Zech. 4:6). We are so full of ourselves, so used to doing it ourselves in our own natural, human strength rather than his resurrection power that we do not know how to lay down control. There is so much to unlearn! Our daily time of prayer is a time of humbling, letting go, releasing us to be powerless and helpless so he can begin to take over.

One of the intercessors in our praying community was sitting at her kitchen table meditating on the Word of God when suddenly a lovely cardinal flew into the windowpane, unaware of the barrier of glass. To her amazement, the bird repeatedly lunged against the pane. The Holy Spirit whispered in her heart, "You are just like that cardinal; you keep plunging ahead in your own strength rather than submitting to my strength. Lean back and rest in me, submit to my authority, and allow me to do whatever needs to be done in my strength, not in yours. You will then be walking in me and not the flesh."

A. W. Tozer in his book *The Pursuit of God* summarizes this truth when he says, "The church waits for the tender voice of the saint who has penetrated the veil and has gazed with inward eye upon the wonder that is God. And yet, thus to penetrate, to push in sensitive living experience into the Holy Presence, is a privilege open to every child of God.

"Why do we consent to abide all our days just outside the Holy of Holies and never enter at all to look upon

God? . . . we fail to draw nigh and the years pass and we grow old and tired in the outer courts of the tabernacle. What hinders us?

"What but the presence of a veil in our hearts? . . . It is the veil of our fleshly, fallen nature continuing to live on unjudged, uncrucified, and unrepudiated. It is the close-woven veil of the self-life, which we have never truly acknowledged, of which we have been secretly ashamed, and which for these reasons we have never brought to the judgment of the cross. It is not too mysterious, this opaque veil, nor is it hard to identify. We have but to look into our own hearts and we shall see it there, sewn and patched and repaired it may be, but there nevertheless, an enemy to our lives and an effective block to our spiritual progress.

"It is woven of the fine threads of the self-life, the hyphenated sins of the human spirit. They are not something we do, they are something we are, and therein lies both their subtlety and their power."[2]

You and I both know that nothing will penetrate the sinful fallen nature of our self-life, our self-love, and self-will but to gaze upon Jesus, our glorious Lord, giving him opportunity to reveal himself to us and cleanse us day by day. The more we see him, the more we love him and want to be more like him and want to be so absorbed in him we forget about ourselves.

Allow the Holy Spirit, who is inside of you, to begin to take more dominion over your inner life. Ask him to be more in charge of your time with him. Let this be a time of mutual sharing in which he speaks to you and you respond and speak to him. Close this book and take five minutes to sit quietly. Then say, "Dear Holy Spirit, I want you to be more real to me. I need you so much. Come and help me. I trust that you will."

You Are Not beyond the Help of God

However deep the pit, God's love is deeper yet.
Corrie ten Boom, The Hiding Place

omma was in a reminiscent mood one evening as she and I talked in the little den in the back of her house. It was a cozy room, a room you knew as you entered was a place of prayer. The little table beside her chair always contained her well-worn Bible and other books she was reading on the devotional life. As we began our conversation I immediately sensed the essence of the hours she had spent in prayer for her children and for many other individuals. The room was dimly lit, but as on scores of our other visits during my lifetime, the brightness of the Holy Spirit shone through Momma as he ministered to both of us.

Since my father's death, Thursday evenings had become a special time to be with Momma. My husband and I always tried to take her out for the evening meal and then spend a little while talking with her when we brought her back to the house. The older she became, the more she spoke about her upbringing in the Midwest and her great yearning for God, even as a child, in the midst of tremendous pain and confusion in her home.

This evening was no exception. My husband, who is a hospital chaplain, was working this particular evening, so Momma and I settled in for our after-dinner conversation. Momma told me that for a long time she had been unaware of how much anger and resentment toward her physically abusive father she had buried. She began to see the effects of that bitterness on her body and spirit. God urged her to lay down all judgment of her earthly father.

"Everywhere I turned in my daily prayer time," she said, "God revealed to me the poison that was spewing out over my life. The damage of that root of bitterness to all of my life was totally encompassing.

"One of the first insights I perceived was, 'Let me help you. There is enough love and power to face your woundedness, to be free, and to be cleansed.' This promise was a persistent message in my heart.

"New insights continued to unfold as he brought me to prayer and the Scriptures, helping me to open my heart to the ministry of the Holy Spirit. Even getting to the point of being able to look at this pain was his work over a long period of time! I wanted to be like Jesus on the cross, saying, 'Father, forgive them, they know not what they do,' but I had been through too much."

After many years of struggling with this entrenchment and with the profoundly crippling memories of abuse,

Momma told me, the Holy Spirit brought her to an encounter with him. This opened the gate so love and forgiveness could wash over her.

"I was praying one day, pouring out all my pain and hurt from the past, and the dear Lord began to rise up in my heart with such love for God the Father. I thought my heart would literally crack open because its depth and magnitude were so overwhelming. In the midst of the washing billows of that love for God, the Holy Spirit began to speak in my spirit saying, 'Is there enough love for God to let some of it spill out on your human father? Is there enough generosity and mercy in that divine love for him to receive some of it?'

"Lord, you know my human love is so battered and shallow, I do not want to give any to him. I'm not sure there is enough left for both of us.

"'My dear precious one,' said Jesus, 'leave your shallow, muddy waters of human love and plunge into this cleansing river of my love for you and your father. There is enough for both of you and lots to spare!'

"I gasped," said Momma. "I drew back in fear, but something said to me, 'It's now or never' and I leaped into that pure holy river of God's love.

"I began to repent and cry out, 'I *do* lay down all judgment and unforgiveness, Jesus, I *do* receive your unconditional love, and I *do* forgive through the power of the blood of Jesus. Cleanse me and fill me with your love; I can't bear this pain any longer!'"

Tears were rolling down both of our faces and our hearts were so aware of the Spirit of Jesus in that room. Momma paused momentarily and then continued, "I began to feel an inner release of such freedom and joy, an avalanche of God's power. It had to be the Romans chapter 8 kind of resurrection power. I was being lifted up from my grave of unforgiveness and judgment, which had nearly buried me and destroyed my body. Old animosities, old hurts began to float away in Jesus' love and compassion. Underground springs that long had been clogged with all kinds of debris began to run free and full in the river of love. I was weeping and singing praises all at the same time; I was released out of a prison house of such darkness and pain. I felt nothing but his peace and joy and saw my father as a precious child of God, wounded, hurt, but being released now to be healed too. By my choice to stop judging him, I no longer held him in a vise of unforgiveness. I was free and so was my father. I knew it in my heart." At the point of being released from unforgiveness the deed was done. God had unlocked the prison door of bitterness, and Momma knew through the revelation of the Holy Spirit that she and her father were free.

Exactly one week later Momma received a letter from her father saying he was dying and asking for her forgiveness for all the pain he had caused. She had not heard from him in years. What a glorious answer to prayer! The words of the prophet Isaiah came to me, "Before they call, I will answer; and while they are yet speaking, I will hear" (Isa. 65:24).

Oh, the power of allowing the love of God to well up in us and wash us clean, releasing the other people involved to begin to respond to Jesus, too. Where there is a "prayer soaked" circumstance, God is allowed greater freedom to redeem a larger portion of the situation. *Prayer soaked* is a term I heard the Reverend Tommy Tyson use years ago. Over the years, this concept has helped us understand the amount of prayer needed in any given situation. Without soaking prayer the one who has forgiven may be released but the other person is not. Have you soaked your situation in prayer to the extent that God is allowed to do what he wants to do? What he wants to do is always more comprehensive than our limited vision allows.

Momma wanted to be sure I understood that her powerful experience came as a result of daily drawing nigh to him, which allows him to draw nigh to us (James 4:8). It was a culmination of seeking, which always results in his coming and helping us, if we will allow him to reveal his life of love within our hearts.

I had never heard this fuller account of her release from years of unforgiveness, but I well remembered when it happened years ago. I had noticed a new freedom and power in her life, a new faith and trust in Jesus. As she was released from her attitudes of bitterness and resentment, the Holy Spirit led her to other struggling persons. In her new sensitivity to the Holy Spirit, she became a channel of the Holy Spirit's life within her.

For someone whose trust level was shattered in childhood to become a person who could trust God so fully was a change only the Holy Spirit could have brought about. But he will do the same in any of us if we are willing to walk in alignment with his nature of love and his Word.

I saw my mother's faith grow to the point that when she prayed, she believed completely that God would act out of his highest good for any situation. This did not come about overnight but slowly, surely, day by day, week by week, year by year as she pored over the Scriptures and began to walk in obedience to the love commandments. My brother, sister, and I saw her grow and mature into a sensitive, compassionate woman of God.

We are all broken and wounded by sin, either our own sin against others and ourselves or their sin against us. Jesus can and will save to the uttermost (Heb. 7:25) if we will respect and submit to his conditions, his way of doing things.

Momma often said, "He is not a respecter of persons but of conditions." The conditions are his commandments or laws and we must move in alignment with them. Daily prayer opens up the life of the Holy Spirit in our spirits, so he can begin to pour out the love of God on us and in us. This outpouring empowers us to walk in obedience to his commandments of love.

I realize there are many degrees of woundedness, some requiring extensive prayer and help, both public and private. But may I say to *anyone* reading this book, no matter how wounded and painful your background, there is a time and place of prayer even for you, where you can come into God's presence as best you can and let him deal with your situation. He is not unreasonable or hard to satisfy; he just yearns for you to come. Do not wait for a more convenient time or circumstance; now is the right time.

As you wait on God to work, ponder the Scriptures, persist, get counseling if necessary, and join a praying community. You will be helped and set free! We are speaking of a lifetime journey, always exciting because he continues to work in us and through us as we yield and submit. All of our victories take time with God. He comes in life-changing episodes to those who are seeking daily, or through the prayers of those who are in earnest. But prayer is essential!

Let me say it again. If my mother could come out of such abuse and harshness to know and experience Jesus' love and healing of emotional barriers, you can too!

Before we leave what God did for Momma, let me share one more story concerning her energetic, faith-filled prayer life. Four days before she died, I was taking care of her on a Thursday night. My sister, who is compassionate and giving, had been at her side earlier in the day. As I sat on the bed with Momma that night, she said, "Margaret, I want you to pray for me and with me out of Matthew 18:19 in agreement that I will be released *soon* to go home to Jesus." She loved that Scripture: "If two of you shall agree on earth as touching any thing that they shall ask, it shall be done for them of my Father which is in heaven." We had seen amazing answers through the years when Momma prayed in agreement with someone concerning a problem.

Struggling with the enormous challenge of loving her deeply as I did and not wanting to see her die, yet knowing it was time for her to be released, I took hold of her hands and asked the Holy Spirit to help me get out of the way. Then I let him pray through me a prayer of release.

"Dear Lord, precious Jesus, Momma wants to come home. We cannot and will not hold her back; we release her into your loving hands. We trust you totally, and we give her into your care. Come, precious Holy Spirit, as we pray in faith believing that you will come soon and take her unto yourself. Thank you Jesus, thank you Father, thank you Holy Spirit." We both knew it was done. I tucked her in bed and left the house in great peace.

Several days passed by, and on Monday morning I called to tell Momma I would be over to take care of her in the evening.

Before our conversation was over she asked, "Are you walking in faith that he is coming for me soon?"

"Yes, Momma, I am."

"Good, it won't be long now. You call me before you come tonight; I may not need you," she answered.

She did not need me. God came that day and took her home.

Once again my mother had demonstrated a great spiritual truth she had discovered about prayer: Real prayer is not the words we say, but the attitude of faith in our hearts long after the audible prayer is over. She used to say, "When we say amen, the real prayer begins!" The "real prayer" is what I trust God to do about the request and whether I truly believe he will act in response to my asking. Momma had great faith because she had seen him do many wonderful things as she trusted him.

If Momma's experience has not convinced you that God can help you, no matter what your past, let me share another story of healing from a woman in our praying community.

Ann is a beloved and radiant Christian today. She is a woman whose prayers always uplift and draw into the presence of Jesus those of us who pray with her each week. She has walked a painful journey of mental illness, but through private and corporate prayer, hours of counseling, medication, her own faith, and the faith of many others, she is filled with light and love today and is leading a victorious life in God.

At one point in Ann's life she had been placed in seclusion because her manic depression had reached uncontrollable levels. For three days and nights she talked incessantly. "I could see out of a small window of my seclusion room," she told me. "Nurses would be passing by, but I was so frightened of being strapped down, I would cry out to God the Father, Son, and Holy Spirit until the nurses would hear me screaming and would come in to try to help me. My husband still remembers the hurt he felt, standing beside my bed, to see me strapped down and in that condition.

"One day the nurses took me to the dining room. I don't remember this, but the nurses said that on the way back to my isolation room I stretched my arms and legs across the door so that they had to struggle to pry me loose. That is how much I didn't want to be in isolation.

"Most of the three days and nights, I had weird dreams. In one of my dreams my father and others who had died with mental illness came to visit me. They encouraged me to hang in there for others and myself. The dreams ended with the voice of my precious aunt calling, 'Ann, Ann.' She is still living and supports me with her love and prayers.

"I became a Christian when I was nine years old, but when I came out of seclusion I saw that many of life's experiences had brought me to my knees in total yieldedness to Jesus. But this dream was truly life changing. At this point I began the journey back to wholeness.

"Today, seventeen years later, I am well, happy, walking daily in the love, joy, and peace of God. My life is one of victory over mental illness. I give God glory for my total healing."

Ann was and continues to be active in daily prayer, waiting and listening for God, and meditating on the Scriptures. She takes care of babies in her home and is a vital and cherished member of our praying community. She has a tremendous understanding of Jesus' reality, brought about by desperate need and much time with God. A consecrated Christian psychiatrist and many praying friends assisted her to wholeness.

As I close this chapter, let me say again: You are not beyond the help of God, if you are willing to let him help you. But you must observe two vital principles demonstrated in both Momma's and Ann's stories.

1. You must be willing to do things God's way. Everyone, no matter the depth of his or her woundedness or mental illness, needs the comforting presence of Jesus released in prayer. There is no quick fix, but he will help you if you allow him to guide you into the network system he has prepared for you. Private and corporate prayer, medical science, supportive family and friends, and the aid of his unspeakable presence will bring you into wholeness.

2. You must persist in seeking him. There are no obstacles to your healing if you are *willing to allow God to help you.*

A man whose wife died before harmony had been restored within their family was angry at her dying. "I'm through with God and with praying," he said. "I feel like God has it in for me. I've tried praying about our family situation. I prayed and our family was not brought together. I'm through; it simply didn't work."

This man did not read the situation as it really was because there were too many needs in his own life. There still can be reconciliation in his family, if family members are willing to own their responsibility and are ready to let God help them. They tried to put God into a box of expected events and conduct, but he will not be forced by any person's prayer. Prayer is not meant to coerce God or others to work as we want them to work. Prayer is rather an unfolding of God's nature of love to change us and release his Holy Spirit to soften the hearts and minds of those in need. Satan is pushed back as we pray so the Holy Spirit can cause those who are being prayed for to make the right choices for good (Luke 11:1–13).

We must be willing to do things in his way.

I believe a failure to persist in the spiritual life is both common and deadly. Many people give up and move on to something they think will be quicker if God does not "perform" at once according to their wishes. It takes persistent praying to begin to discover how much prayer it takes to release God's power!

A young man came into our praying community a few years ago, wanting to give prayer a "try" for a year. After this trial year he announced, "I've tried this prayer thing for a year now. I think I will take next year to improve my golf game, so I won't be coming anymore."

He was unable to perceive the magnitude of his need. He was giving God one year and had poor skills in learning *how* to receive from God. His view was too limited to understand God's way of working, and he did not persist long enough to begin truly to love God. He wanted to put his prayer card in the slot and pull out the answer pronto, but he was so focused on self, he could not allow God to be God! Submitting to God's laws was too difficult.

God never forces. He ever seeks to draw (John 6:44). Our part, which I will speak of later, is to learn how to receive him and his empowerment.

The glorious good news is that no one is hopeless or beyond God's grace. He has his ways and we learn the

hows and whys of his ways as we meet him daily in waiting, listening, and prayerful submission to his authority.
Instead of thinking, "Lord, I am through with you," begin
to think, "Lord, I've been trying to do this my way in my
understanding. Now I open the door to the Holy Spirit
showing me your love and your compassion, your pattern of helping me."

Will you put this book down now and say, "Father, I am
going to draw as close to you as I can and ask the Holy
Spirit to give me your wisdom and insight into my situation. What would you have me do? By your grace I will
persist until the answer comes and continue to meet you
daily and walk in obedience by your grace. Help me,
Jesus."

His Love
Seeks Us Out

To love Him is not to seek Him longer; but to accept Him who has long been seeking us.

Starr Daily

I was once privileged to hear Starr Daily, the onetime hardened criminal, tell of his first meeting with Jesus Christ. Starr has gone to heaven now, but I will never forget hearing him describe how Jesus entered his dungeon of darkness and despair.[3]

Starr had been shoved down into a pit, a "hole" where incorrigible prisoners were kept in hope that solitude would cause them to "break." Full of hatred and anger, with no feelings of remorse for the crimes he had committed, he spent his first days of confinement building and refining plots of revenge to carry out should he ever be released from captivity.

Starr had been in the "hole" for some time when suddenly he became aware of another Presence in the small space with him. Slowly Jesus' face, which he recognized instantly, turned towards him. The love-filled, penetrating eyes of Christ, compassionate and pure, looked deeply into his eyes.

"My gaze was fixed," said Starr. "I could do nothing but look into the eyes that commanded my attention. I saw immediately such unbelievable love for me. I was held in their embrace of unconditional love.

"That love began to roll over me, and out beyond me to every harsh and terrible thing that had been done to me, and on to every miserable, terrible thing I had done to hurt anyone else. As I looked, my heart was melted down to the bare essentials of realizing that truly Jesus loves me! I was treasured, cherished, loved by Calvary love, for He had gone to the cross for me.

"I threw my heart and mind around Him, I bowed before Him, as He loved me into His very life of love. We embraced in my spirit, and every need was filled by His love. The pain of every hurt and every wound was assuaged as His love saturated my whole being. I was whole, I was healed and I was well for the first time in my life.

"He didn't leave me, He stayed with me in the 'hole' and it became the secret place of the most high God," said Starr.

When Starr was finally released from solitary confinement, he was transformed but realized he had a long journey to make to be like Jesus. He had been born again and filled with the Spirit of love, the Holy Spirit, poured out by Jesus. "I knew," said Starr, "that I was setting out on the greatest adventure in my life and indeed it has been!"

Starr Daily's adventure included learning to let Jesus be the dominant personality in their relationship, to yield his self-will to God, to live humbly, and to let Jesus live his life through him. Jesus did live within Starr Daily. His life was a vessel through which Jesus loved others.

Jesus' love seeks us out. No matter where our journey may take us, if someone is praying for us, the Holy Spirit is released to act. And Luke 11:13 assures us that he will come to us: "If ye then, being evil, know how to give good gifts unto your children, how much more shall your heavenly Father give the Holy Spirit to them that ask him."

Through years of intensive and sacrificial prayer on the part of Starr's parents and the woman who would become his wife, the release of the Holy Spirit brought Starr to profound repentance and confession of his sins. In the presence of Jesus, he saw and experienced God's love for him and truly was made whole.

We do not have to have the same experience of God's holy love that Starr Daily had. God customizes every situation because we are all handmade. God knew what Starr needed to bring him to himself: Only when Starr was helpless, able to do nothing in the "hole," was Jesus able to attract his attention. Then Starr was ready to receive him through the ministry of God's love and come to repentance and purifying confession.

God's Commitment

As God's love seeks us out, his commitment is threefold.

1. He comes with his love to our hearts. We can only know some truths through experience. We can, in fact, only know them by firsthand encounter. God's love is one such truth. We must receive it through personal experience to truly know it is ours. Whether the experience is dramatic is irrelevant. What matters is the authenticity of God's presence as he relates to you or me. Romans 5:5 says, "the love of God is shed abroad in our hearts by the Holy Spirit." When he comes, he comes to stay, never to leave us or forsake us (Heb. 13:5). He brings all that he is, and all that he is remains in our spirits. The Holy Spirit *is* the love of God.

We can read about this satisfying, loving friendship all our life, and even give it mental assent. But only as the Holy Spirit takes up residency in our hearts and we come away to be with him daily can we begin to fellowship with him and know experientially that the thrill of his presence is more wondrous than any words can describe.

A significant difference exists between theorizing about God's love and actually receiving it. This difference is as obvious as the difference between talking to a starving person about food and giving that person food to eat.

In rebirth Jesus enters our spirits and forgives our sins, and we are brought into the family of God. God's essence when he enters our hearts is holy, unconditional, everlasting love, and we have no understanding of its scope. The promise of the Father, the Holy Spirit, has entered into our sinful, feeble human life (Acts 1:4–5, 8). The far-reaching consequences of this event will begin to unfold as we learn to live with him and he with us.

No matter how memorable or magnificent our rebirth experience was or how fantastic being filled with the Holy Spirit may have been, these experiences are the beginning, not the climax, of this friendship. This friendship will know no limits of communion if we allow the Holy Spirit to take his rightful place and be the initiator of our inner life with him. To learn to stay as yielded as when we received him is one of the challenges of time spent with him (Col. 2:6–10).

God has a monumental task laid out before him, for he must train us to give him our fullest cooperation. Without this involvement we do not learn to move with him in responding to his love and grace. We can frustrate his grace, as Paul explains in Galatians 2:21, so that his movements toward us cannot be fully helpful due to our resisting him or hindering what he wants to do. In our humanity, we are unaware of what he is seeking to tell us and be within us. The nature of God's love is so foreign, so contrary to human love, and yet so perfectly suited to our deepest needs that we need enormous amounts of exposure to it. He wants to activate his love as we spend time with him, so we become sensitive to his personhood.

This activation of his presence can happen anywhere or at any time. Returning home from an errand today, I was in need of trusting Jesus immediately in a particular situation, and I cried aloud to him in the privacy of my car. In that moment of distress he caused his love for me to wash over my spirit and I knew that he loved me. Then I heard him say in my heart, "Trust me, trust me, trust what I have said to you out of my Word in the past about this situation."

As I heard him say those words of assurance his love for me quickened faith once again. I knew he was in control of this circumstance, and I once again rested in him!

Jesus delights to come to us with his heavenly love.

2. He comes to stay. Jesus has promised to stay with us and never to abandon us (Heb. 13:5). He is always there whether I "feel" him or not.

A constant threat to believing that God is always present is that we allow our emotions or mental state to dictate God's position. All too often we determine the state of his "presence" or "absence" on what our emotions are telling us at the time. Thus we let our emotions, rather than our belief in what he has said in his Word, dictate to us.

The Bible tells us that God's residence in our spirit or heart is permanent. He longs to teach us how to meet him there. As we meditate on his Word, our minds will be brought under his loving control, and we will learn not to lean on our emotions.

He is always present to us, even when we wrongly perceive he is absent or when Satan tells us he is absent.

Great writers of the past have said, "What we feel to be
his absence is really his presence."

Deep parts of us do not want his intimacy because we
do not trust this strange yet wonderful love. We run from
him to the security of what we have known and are able
to control. The Holy Spirit must lead us into deeper experiences of his love, and as he does, we learn that his love
can be trusted. We cannot take much of him at first
because our capacity to receive him is so shallow. But
the blessed Holy Spirit, who is the love of God, will begin
from the moment he first comes to lead us into more and
more of what Ephesians 3:16–19 describes: "He would
grant you according to the riches of his glory, to be
strengthened with might by his Spirit in the inner man;
that Christ may dwell in your hearts by faith; that ye,
being rooted and grounded in love, may be able to comprehend with all saints what is the breadth, and length,
and depth, and height; and to know the love of Christ,
which passeth knowledge, that ye might be filled with all
the fulness of God."

3. He is always available and eager to be our friend.
Another delightful discovery in the life of prayer and waiting on God is that he is more available, more accessible,
and more eager than we are to build a loving, intimate
friendship. He keeps drawing and drawing us; he never
gives up. It simply is not possible to articulate with
human vocabulary the experiential depth of the wonder
and unbelievable dimensions of God's love which he ever
and increasingly brings to us in the life of prayer. We have
no way to comprehend the precious intimacy, the unend-
ing acceptance into our Beloved's life of love, the companionship which protects the door of our heart from
the pain of human isolation and loneliness. He is so eager
to be with us that he will give us a growing ability to be
responsive to his presence of love. In our times alone
with him, day after day, we learn how to receive his love.

The eternal truth remains that he wants to be with us more than we want to be with him. Though he is willing and waiting patiently for time with us, it must be private, undisturbed time for the communication to begin.

After many years of observing the life of God in others and in myself, I am firmly convinced that no matter how he comes into our hearts, whether through a life-changing experience of rebirth or a quiet experience of baptism in the Holy Spirit, no matter what dimension of God's love his Spirit sheds abroad in our spirits, it is his purpose to pour out his love increasingly in each and every believer. The Holy Spirit has been given for this very purpose! It is his presence, his love, which empowers us to be his witnesses, unto Jerusalem, in all Judea and in Samaria and unto the uttermost parts of the earth (Acts 1:8)!

First John 4:16 says, "we have *known* [experientially] and *believed* [trusted] the love that God hath to us" (emphasis added). Knowing and trusting are lifetime experiences and are fed by the underground springs of God's love in our devotional time. We must daily allow the Holy Spirit freedom to draw us more and more to the eternal, everlasting love of God.

There is a secret place of the Most High, an abiding place where the great protection of his love spreads his wings over us. We are infused with his divine, holy love as we wait on him, as we linger and listen, as we ask the Holy Spirit to make alive his written Word. But that takes a commitment on our part.

Our Commitment

No relationship in the human realm is satisfying if it is one-sided. This fact is also true in our relationship with the Trinity. In the previous section we established the nature of God's commitment in this spiritual relationship. Now let's look at the commitment you and I need to make to continue living in the promise of the Father. Our commitment consists of four significant challenges.

 1. We must establish a place to meet him. We can form new habits to enhance our relationship with the Trinity and in the process develop practical ways to lay down control. Scripture reminds us that we can ask God to meet every need (Phil. 4:6). Begin by asking the Holy Spirit to help you find a place in your home where you will have the fewest interruptions as you endeavor to spend time with him. It should be a quiet place, where the television and telephone can be silenced and the family will not interrupt you when you are praying, except for emergencies.

It is important for your family to know God is precious enough to you to be given a "sanctuary" in your home. A pleasant, quiet place where you sit at his feet is the best testimony of his significance to you. "This is where Mother prays," or "This is where Dad talks to God," your spouse and children will say, giving powerful testimony to your love and devotion to him.

To establish a regular place of prayer helps to confirm the time of prayer and keeps the atmosphere of that place reverent and peaceful. Many people are establishing prayer corners or prayer nooks in their homes. Others have prayer chairs or places on the couch where they pray regularly, and children in the home can be taken there to be loved and held as well as to be prayed for.

Children need to begin to establish quiet places in their rooms as well. They can be encouraged to read their Bibles and develop primary prayer patterns that will get them in touch with Jesus.

My mother had a chair in her bedroom with her Bible and books on prayer close by. We children knew to play quietly when she was talking with God. I often tucked myself into that chair when she was out of the room, feeling great solace and help because I knew God visited her there.

I am aware that in homes where there are children, times and places for prayer are more challenging to establish. But even in difficult settings the Holy Spirit has a way to lead you into more prayer. He has a pattern of prayer that will work uniquely in your home. He is also able to take unexpected interruptions and turn them into significant times of prayer.

A young mother I know, who rises thirty minutes before her family awakens, found one morning that one of her children had followed her to her prayer chair. She drew him up on her lap and they prayed together for a while. Then he nodded off to sleep and she held him in her arms as she prayed silently. We know that Susannah Wesley's signal to her children that she wanted a moment for quiet prayer was to throw her apron over her head. These times alone with God provided wonderful visual teaching for her children.

Ask God to help you discover a special place to meet with him.

2. We must establish a time to meet him. The devotional life is the secret to God's unfolding his love nature to us in all his beauty and power (Ps. 63:2). He begins to draw us into a deeper relating, a wider capacity to receive him, as we open our time to him. When he begins to be important enough to us, we will devote every opportunity to allow him to take over more within us and reveal himself to us. He has to teach us everything, from how to relate to his invisible presence, to picking up on his inner promptings, to knowing the difference between his voice (God says) and our voice (I say).

So the great issue in the devotional life is *how?* How do we give the Holy Spirit the kind of time and undivided attention he needs to reveal himself in us? How does he reveal God's love to us as he alone can do?

How do the rivers of living water with their crystal clear, pure heavenly love (John 7:37–39) begin to overflow their banks into our lives of lovelessness? How do we begin to wade into the rivers of God's love (Ps. 36:8), not only up to the ankles, as Ezekiel 47 states, not even only up to the knees nor up to the loins, but to the point where we are swimming in it? Ezekiel 47:9 suggests that everything will live wherever the river flows! God's love, and his love alone, brings healing and wholeness of life because these waters of God issue out of the sanctuary, God's very throne, says Revelation 22:1.

There are depths of God's love we will only know in heaven, when all sin is removed. But in this earthly state something happens to people hungry enough to linger in God's presence, unhurried, sitting at his feet, gazing at him, waiting, listening for his word as Mary did (Luke 10:38–42). Everyone I know who is sitting at his feet is experiencing a growing depth of his divine love, as it pours lavishly and extravagantly from his heart. Any and all who are willing, privately and corporately, to give him access, to sit at his feet, to ponder his Word, to wait on him, to yield to him, will find him. And they will be empowered to allow him to work in them, to change their wills and their actions (Phil. 2:13).

The secret lies then in giving him time to speak through Scripture, in giving him entrance into all sectors of our inner life, and in being trained by him to receive his love. There is much to unlearn, but once he begins to invade and permeate all our heart's affections, he penetrates all our mental and emotional attitudes.

Ask the Holy Spirit to guide you in establishing a time to meet with him. He will guide you in opening up the time that is best for you. If you try on your own to set a time that is right, you will vacillate between many options. The secret to all decisions is to turn at once to the Holy Spirit and ask him to reveal to you his will. He will do so. Often the answer will come with amazing speed and simplicity. If you try to work out a meeting time, it will fail. If you allow him to establish your time together, it will succeed.

Our heavenly Father is reasonable, not demanding more than we can do. He knows our frame, says Psalm 103:14. He knows we are made out of the dust of the earth. He understands our need for rest and our need for him. I have found that when I ask for his way of doing things, he empowers me to obey and goes ahead of me to make the way clear.

At one turning point in my life I asked God to help me establish a time with him. The response came clearly: "I want you to begin having a time alone with me each day where we can begin to be in conversation with each other." He encouraged me to rise an hour earlier each day for this special time.

The following morning I went to my place of prayer from six to seven o'clock. This pattern remained with me for many years. Patterns of prayer will change with the seasons of life. God draws us into more and more prayer the older we become as we are willing to pray all through the day (1 Thess. 5:17).

Turning to the indwelling Holy Spirit and asking him to guide you in the way he wants gives control and leadership to him, rather than to our own human effort. In fact, laying down our enormous control and self-assertiveness is the whole issue of time with God. He teaches us how to do it in our time with him.

Let me illustrate. One morning after spending considerable time in the Scriptures and prayer, I got up to go about the tasks of the day. After all, I am a busy person! But the Holy Spirit said, "Sit down, you are not yielded to me yet. After all this time in my presence you are still in control!"

The minute I heard the Holy Spirit, I knew he was speaking the truth. Oh yes, I was leaning toward him, wanting him to be in control, but I was still fixed in my will, still not surrendered to him and his life in me. I had not truly given him my day to live as he wanted to live it in me. I was still in control and exhibiting strong self-will!

I sat down. I wish words were adequate to describe what took place in the next ten to fifteen minutes. First, Jesus brought all the events of the day to mind, in order. To the best of my ability (which is all he asks) I laid down what I thought should be done or said and opened up the entire day to him, saying, "Lord, I surrender to what you want to do or say. I lay down all control, all self-will. You do through me whatever you want to do."

I let go. I submitted to him, and he helped me to release everything I had held on to that day. I felt as if a cleansing tidal wave had washed over me. When I got up from my chair, I was in him and he was activated in me. His will, not mine, could be done that day. What an amazing day it was, and so full of him. A dear friend of mine would say, "You laid down your yoke for his yoke" (Matt. 11:28–30).

3. We need to relax and receive him. Becoming aware of the indwelling Holy Spirit is not something I can force or produce through any effort of my own (John 6:63). It is a gift from him. Each day as I take my place in his presence, I take a deep breath and relax, let go, and slow down, so that all agitation leaves me. So often we come to our time and place with him nervous, upset, out of touch. We cry out, asking him to give us the reality of his calming presence. The tension of striving and straining will surface often during our time with him, and we will need repeatedly to slow down, relax again, take another deep breath, and let go, to cast our burdens on him and learn to leave them there. Isaiah 30:15 says, "In returning and rest shall ye be saved; in quietness and in confidence shall be your strength."

I love my intentional time with Jesus because his Spirit teaches me to rest in him, to look upon him and realize afresh his marvelous grace and power, which are always available to me (Eph. 1:17–23). One day after a time of meditation in the Scripture and relaxing in his presence I heard him say in my heart, "Margaret, I really appreciate the fact that you are trying to be more dependent on me. There is less striving in your own strength and you are relaxed more in your time with me. But do you see what is happening?"

"No, Lord, I don't."

"You *are* letting go more. But letting go of some control has triggered insecurities in you because not knowing what I might do next causes you to be anxious."

I saw it as he spoke and began to laugh at myself. How funny we are! I felt a lightness within that he too saw the humor of it all. Yet I did not feel any condemnation from him.

Thank God for a place of prayer in your home, and for a time set aside daily to fellowship with God. How wonderful it is to know that when we get there we do not have to do *anything* but relax and tune in to him. He is in charge. Our place is to submit and learn to follow, to respond to him. Only the Holy Spirit can bring into focus this time with God.

As we relax, surrendering our hearts to him, this very yielding allows us to receive his loving presence.

4. We must be willing to allow the Holy Spirit to shift us from self-focus to God-focus. As I linger in the presence of the Holy Spirit and he begins to illumine Jesus to me, I begin to see the vast difference between Jesus and me. I see Jesus being dependent on Father God (John 5:19, 30), while I see myself thinking I can handle things in my own strength. What audacity to believe that I have the resources within myself to handle life's situations when Jesus was dependent on God. If Jesus was dependent on his Father, how much more should I submit to the authority of God? Customarily I "take over" out of the "I" consciousness in every area of my life. Seeking God's counsel first is foreign to me, whether in his written Word or in prayerful waiting on him. My assertive, strong-willed assumption is that I am knowledgeable about the whats and hows of doing nearly everything. Such a shift in control means I must lay down my self-reliance and self-confidence, which are entrenched from years and years of practice. I will have to renounce my "best of the flesh" actions and responses that pervade every part of my being. I must own my tendency to "do it myself" in my carnal, soulish energy; I must learn to speak of my limitations and tendencies without being defensive or protective of my selfishness.

As I am able to shift focus through the Holy Spirit's power, he will sensitize me to walking in humble, lowly dependence on him. He desires to teach me how helpless I truly am. He wants me to lay down at Jesus' feet the burden of taking full responsibility for everything. I must refuse to move out on my own in any way and wait, instead, to do only what Jesus reveals in our time together (John 5:19, 30).

Of course, this new relationship with the Spirit does not excuse us from being responsible. We do need to go to work, pay bills, and take out the trash! Nevertheless, in spending time with God we move into an inner journey of being helpless and dependent.

A great mystery begins to unfold as we assimilate into our daily living the reality of the indwelling presence of the Holy Spirit. As we take the humble and lowly place, giving him the place of control, we move more and more into who we are in him. We are becoming less like our old, sinful, fallen selves and more like the persons he designed us to be (Matt. 16:24–26)! In this case less is truly more; less of me reveals more of him as I come into all I am in him. What an amazing paradox (1 Peter 5:6)!

He Comes as Teacher

> "But the Comforter, which is the Holy Ghost, whom the Father will send in my name, he shall teach you all things, and bring all things to your remembrance, whatsoever I have said."
>
> *John 14:26*

The Scriptures tell us that one of the principal ways the Holy Spirit functions in our lives is as our teacher. As I unfold my understanding of the Spirit's teaching role, I would like to share an incident from my life that portrays this role in a profound way.

One evening I attended a gathering also attended by a woman who for over ten years had received much prayer and concern from all of us. She had given God entrance into her life in amazing ways and had begun walking in humility and obedience.

She was a leader in the community, so the results of her new commitment to God were noted by literally hundreds of people. Many of us continued in earnest, travailing prayer for her, and she continued to walk in increasing trust in God.

But on this occasion I found her, to my dismay and grief, not on a resting plateau, in and out of which we all vacillate from time to time, but in a defiant reversal of any progress she had made, a real denial of Jesus. The return of her rebellion was even worse than before (Luke 11:21–26). She had regressed to a life where her self-will was in control rather than the newly embraced will of God. Those of us who had been praying for her were shocked and saddened by what we saw that night; it was a decided turning back.

As I drove home later, I was confused and disturbed. Over and over in my head and my heart rang one question: Lord, what has happened?

I knew full well the power of the enemy in the midst of any prayer endeavor. All of us who were praying knew Satan would show his hand, and he had many times over the years only to be defeated time after time. As a professional therapist, I knew the treachery of unresolved personal issues in the hand of the enemy, issues of self-worth, control, and power, needs for acceptance, pride, and self-bias. Each of these presents an open battlefield that Satan loves to enter. Once there, he darkens an individual's understanding through unawareness and ignorance, often filling him or her with false answers (Eph. 4:17–20).

So eager was our friend to get her needs met that she chose Satan's flattering answers of quick success, rather than allowing the Holy Spirit into her problem spots with his life-giving answers. I had been aware of the potential quicksand in these emotional arenas of her life, but her needs for love and acceptance were greater than any of us realized. Now my questions were, Had we failed? and What should we do now? God had so clearly called us to pray for her.

I parked in our driveway, pulled out the key, and headed toward the house in enormous spiritual pain. Years and years of serious corporate and private prayer—scriptural prayer, impassioned weeping, and faith-believing prayer—for this woman flashed through my memory. That prayer had cost us something in rest, pleasure, time, and food. That prayer was not cheap, easy, or casual, but intentional, dedicated intercession on the part of many people.

I entered our home and went right to my place of prayer. Passionately I cried out, "Jesus, help me, teach me. I've got to understand what is going on, what you are allowing to happen, what you want us to do now. I know I need to be on a purer level of love and faith. I submit to you at every level. Reveal whatever you need to reveal, show me where I am out of your will. I repent. You can say whatever you want to say, and I will receive it and walk in obedience! I've done the best I can for where I am."

I realized that God's plan for this person remained the same. His allowing our friend's backsliding caused me, in a moment of revelation, to see where she was on her spiritual journey. What, I wondered, should my response be? Had I misinterpreted something? Help me, God, to see anew where I need to pray and how to do it.

Even as I prayed, my heart and mind tumbled over each other in an attempt to get to God, to hear his side of the situation. I knew I needed God's answer, God's plan, not human understanding. Our precious heavenly Father wanted to teach me what he needed me to do. Without his response, I could only throw up my hands in discouragement and abandon what he had called into being.

Psalm 62:8 says, "Pour out your heart before him," and that is exactly what I was doing. I was so grieved over this dear person losing her way. Why had God not answered our fervent prayers?

My mother often said, "Where the answer is delayed in coming, or very slow to come, there are several possible reasons." First, she suggested, we need to examine ourselves and see where we are in disobedience of any kind, and particularly in the area of lovelessness toward anyone. Disobedience of Jesus' love commandments is the basic reason for unanswered prayer (John 13:34–35; 15:9–10, 12).

A second reason for delayed answers may be that we are praying out of our own stubborn self-will more than we realize, and not in the will of God. We are not in touch with the Holy Spirit within, who will reveal God's will (Rom. 8:26–27). I will develop this later.

Third, God may be working out far deeper and more extensive divine purposes than we can imagine, purposes which take considerably more time to bring about.

As I wept and prayed, trying unsuccessfully to get quiet, I heard nothing from God. I simply could not get past my emotional pain to hear his still, small voice. I persisted for two hours until just after midnight, when I heard our front door open. It was my husband coming home from work.

"What are you doing up at this hour?" he asked as he came down the hall. "Why aren't you in bed?"

How I longed to pour out to him the whole situation. But in my spirit I felt the restraint of the Holy Spirit. "Don't talk to anyone about this, even to John, until you have heard from me," said the still, small voice of God.

He was saying, in other words, that I was to keep my concern secret and silent from any human flesh, no matter how comfortable and dear, until the Lord God had spoken in instruction and understanding. I am your teacher, he reminded me.

How often the intensity with which we need to wait until we hear from God is defused and weakened when we allow the best of human spiritual understanding to speak to us. We need, instead, to continue to seek after him until he truly answers the way he wants, and needs, to answer!

So I told John, "I was just sitting in the quiet, listening and waiting." And John began to share with me about his day.

I slept well and awakened early the next morning. When I slipped away to my prayer place, I was calmer, more subdued. How it helps to pour out our hearts, even if he does not respond at once in the way we would like him to respond. Getting our troubles off our hearts vocally causes us to become quiet and relaxed. I knew he would respond to my heart's cry when the time was right, but not when I was too agitated to hear anything. The great saints of all the ages have spoken of the need for "emptying out" or a *kenosis* of all we may be feeling so we *can* be receptive in a calm manner to hear God speak (Phil. 2:5–8).

More refreshed, quiet, but still hurting terribly over what seemed to me a huge failure, I came again into his presence. I opened the Scriptures to the Psalms, reading and reading as these words ministered to me.

After nearly an hour and a half I laid the Bible down and sat quietly and peacefully in Jesus' presence, knowing he does all things well. As I waited, I was uplifted by his loving nearness, and he began to teach me what was happening. He reminded me that prayer cannot coerce another person's will or his will. Prayer releases the working of the Holy Spirit to bring about the will of God. And when profound purposes are involved, it takes time for God to work them out. What I saw at first as a reversal, God allowed me to see as a detour in the general scheme of things. I was reminded once again of George Mueller, who prayed for fifty-two years for five people who came to God only after he died. God was teaching our prayer group to persist until the answer came, not knowing how long that might be.

As God's revelation came in clarity and force I felt compelled to make a written account of it, for fear I could not retain it. "What is won by prayer must be maintained by prayer," the Holy Spirit told me. "There has been sacrificial prayer over a long period of time, prayer that has truly cost all of you something for years. That level of prayer needs to continue and to intensify. The forces of evil are escalating as never before, and only fasting and prayer will push back the enemy, so I have freedom to draw this one, for whom you have great concern, unto Jesus. You must realize that great spiritual forces are drawn against this answer, but I have heard your prayers, and will answer. But again, you must intensify your sacrificial praying.

"Second, you are going to have to trust me as you never have before. You are too shattered by what you saw last night, and too easily stricken by outer circumstances, which means you need to know me more intimately and trust my character regardless of the external manifestations."

Second Corinthians 4:15–18 came to mind and I remembered how my mother refused to express any doubt or unbelief after praying over a situation. Her faith would not allow her to express discontent with what God was doing or how he brought the answer about. The Holy Spirit showed me that the longer we pray over a situation the more activated our faith must be to trust what he has said to us in prayer.

Third, the Holy Spirit revealed that the forces of the enemy had deceived the one for whom we were praying through the depth of her personal need. She could get her ego needs met quickly if she allowed herself to please others, and she had succumbed to this powerful temptation (John 5:44). We were to continue praying for those personal needs and believe that in God's own time and way she would respond to him.

Finally, the Holy Spirit indicated that we were to magnify our praying over any and all people in similar situations, so we would not get fixated on our particular situation but would include all persons in the same predicament. We were to lift them up to Jesus, even as we lifted our situation, by faith believing that God's power would be activated in each and every setting. He continues to teach us to pray larger, bigger prayers, trusting him to move out in power.

A real peace welled up in me as the indwelling Spirit not only laid out what he wanted us to do in prayer but made it clear we must continue in his love and compassion, trusting him until the victory comes.

We are in the process of praying as God instructed, and we are staying close to him so he can continue to teach us what we need to learn. Our faith is high for the final answer. He has given us unchangeable confidence that he will bring the woman involved back to himself, and we believe him. "For I will hasten my word to perform it" (Jer. 1:12).

God's Commitment

1. He comes to teach us. One of the most significant aspects of the depth of God's unconditional love is that he himself, in the person of the Holy Spirit, comes to help us. And one of his most crucial helps is his teaching. As he teaches us, we come to better understand his nature and what he is seeking to do in and for us. He will reveal the truth of all situations, helping us to interpret them correctly and view events as he does (1 Cor. 2:9–16; Prov. 2:6).

It is not only through impressions in our thought processes that God reveals his truth to us. He also teaches from his presence living in our hearts and speaking to us from our human spirit. He activates the Scriptures as we ponder over them. As we continue to wait, the Holy Spirit brings us understanding and knowledge. If we will draw nigh to him and wait on him, we can be assured that he will come to us. John 14:26 says, "But the Comforter, which is the Holy Spirit, whom the Father will send in my name [the promise of the Father], *he shall teach you all things*" (emphasis added). Speaking of Jesus, Isaiah 11:2 says, "And the spirit of the LORD shall rest upon him, the spirit of wisdom and understanding, the spirit of counsel and might, the spirit of knowledge and the fear of the LORD."

God loves to teach us through the work of the indwelling Holy Spirit, the source of teaching within us. He is the utterly reliable source of all truth in any given situation if we really want to hear from him. The promise of the Father is that he is our teacher.

God's interpretation is nearly always radically different from mine, especially since I tend to read situations selfishly and with self-will and control issues. As he teaches me the accurate perception, the truth, because he is the Spirit of truth (John 14:17), I learn to pray more fully in God's will (James 4:3) and not to pray amiss. (We will discuss this in more depth later.) Isaiah 55:8–9 says, "My thoughts are not your thoughts, neither are your ways my ways, saith the LORD."

It takes more time than we like to admit to have the mind of Christ (1 Cor. 2:16). In reality, few people give God adequate time to convey his wisdom; as a result, many have the mistaken idea he is not interested in communicating with us. But he longs to communicate with us. He will as we learn to be more responsive to the indwelling Holy Spirit. We miss so much of what he is saying now because we will not give the daily time necessary to learn to know his sweet voice.

What comfort to know that he will draw nigh as our teacher. He will and does respond to our heart's cry for insight and understanding. He will teach us; he will illumine us with heavenly wisdom and knowledge as we allow him opportunity.

2. He gently reveals self-knowledge. The Holy Spirit, our teacher, reveals to us the inner workings of our minds, wills, and emotions. Yet he is so tender, so kind, that the depth of that revelation, that self-knowledge, will only be what I can bear (Mark 4:33). "Thou desirest truth in the inward parts: and in the hidden part thou shalt make me to know wisdom" (Ps. 51:6). He shares such love as he helps me see myself that I feel blessed, cherished, treasured. If I feel condemned, I know Satan has entered in, wanting to produce self-condemnation. One of the most amazing inner ministries of the Holy Spirit is that he will so strengthen me in his nature that I can learn to stand against the accusation of Satan's forces. Only he can reveal how this is to be. It is unique for each one of us. I refuse the enemy permission to accuse an accepted child of God (Rom. 8:1–2).

Saint Teresa of Avila says, "Some people are so blind . . . that when a trial strikes them, they complain to God, 'What have I done to deserve this?', the implication being that they have done nothing, that they are innocent of a great deal of inner disorder lurking in their minds and hearts."[4] The inner, loving workings of the Holy Spirit, the promise of the Father, will help me begin to look, through his great love, at my poverty of soul and spirit. And I will find the quality of my need staggering.

Late one afternoon a man whom I had been counseling said to me in great anger, "I don't think your decision on this subject was right! I challenge your conclusion, and I don't like it." My decision had been painful to reach, but after much prayer and thought I had felt persuaded it was right. I understood the conflict it had set up in this man's heart, but he had not come against it in our talks before.

"You certainly need to come to your own conclusions," I replied. "You asked what I felt and I told you." His sudden anger surprised me, and although I felt uneasiness regarding his choices, I knew he had to decide to do right. I could not do it for him.

Several days went by. I found myself feeling tremendously impatient over his outburst, but in times with God, I was aware only of the man's woundedness as he spoke angrily to me. But one morning as I meditated on the Scriptures, the Holy Spirit said, "Margaret, this man did speak out of woundedness, but your response was also one of pride and impatience. You were every bit as wrong as he was."

I saw at once my defensiveness. Even though I had spent much time with God, I was not ready until a couple of days later to allow him to teach me and reveal my hidden self to me. But as God spoke to me through his Word, illumined by the Holy Spirit, he was able to help me. I repented deeply on the spot and acknowledged that my woundedness is as dark as everyone else's. I humbled myself to speak the truth of my sin of impatience and anger to this man.

Our Commitment

As we begin a pilgrimage in God's presence, that which we need most is the area of our greatest deficiency. By this I mean that our assessment of our true condition and recognition of how much we need him is highly inadequate. This is fine, because at this early stage we are not able to look too closely at our need; our sense of need, which causes us to be more open to him, will grow the more we linger in his presence. The beginning of this time with God is the most difficult, then, since we seem to be overflowing with ourselves, afraid to let go and unaccustomed to letting our lives be lived in touch with the indwelling Holy Spirit.

1. We need to present our levels of openness and teachability to God. Proverbs 3:5–7 says, "Lean not unto thine own understanding. In all thy ways acknowledge him, and he shall direct thy paths. . . . Be not wise in thine own eyes."

We can have the greatest teacher in the world, which we have, but if we are so full of ourselves that we are unwilling to allow him access to us, we will not profit from his masterful instruction.

We have been using a word repeatedly in this book, and it holds the key to being teachable or open to the Holy Spirit. The word is *allow,* and I have used the word each time in reference to allowing the Holy Spirit to be who he is. Mother Teresa of Calcutta invites us to "give God permission" to be all he is to each of us.

The more contact we have with the Holy Spirit, the more his presence begins to soften and empower us to see our desperate need of him. His compassion will not allow our growing sense of need to be overwhelming.

It is permissible to begin with whatever level of teachableness you have. Where you are now is the result of the inner silent work of the Holy Spirit to the extent you have allowed him. He will draw you more and more into facing, with him, your helplessness, your emptiness. The great saints have taught for centuries that he brings about an awareness of our neediness in order that we might be open to him.

I believe our spirits are meant to be as open to God as they can be so we can have the most satisfying relationships possible.

2. We must begin to wait on God. We enter a whole new realm of responsive receptivity not out of personality or the power of self-will but out of our human spirits as we humbly ask the Holy Spirit to teach us how to wait quietly on God to allow him to manifest his presence. We need to listen for him, letting him be the initiator in our relationship (Isa. 40:28–31).

Many Christians feel that time with God should be an almost ceaseless flow of talking to and at him. Back of much of our constant talking to God is our feeling that he must see our point of view and do things our way. We think we must convince him of the best thing to do. We think that if our self-effort and self-will are strong enough, he will have to bend to our way of thinking.

In this latter part of the twentieth century we are overdeveloped in the soulish realm; our emotions, minds, and wills rule us. We have been trained in competency and skills of all kinds and think we should bring that fleshly power into our times with God. We feel secure, or at least familiar, with our human drive to succeed; our talents and education all say, "Go out there and do it; take over and get the job done." We are self-reliant, self-realized, and highly independent, or worse, self-dependent.

We are used to taking over out of our best human judgment, but to be truly dependent on God within us is often unheard of, even in the most enlightened Christian circles. We are expected to act out of human maturity tinged with a generalized blessing from God.

To allow the indwelling Spirit of Jesus to be activated within us means we cease all conversation, quietly asking the Holy Spirit to teach us to be still, responsive, attentive to him. Each day we wait patiently for him to make the initial step toward us (Prov. 8:34–36).

The power of our self-effort and self-will make taking the humble, lowly place before him difficult, nearly impossible; but the Holy Spirit honors in an unusual way any gesture of submitting to him in our devotional life (Isa. 25:9). This leads us to see a powerful spiritual law:

To the degree I submit to him in the place of prayer, to that degree will I be yielded to him in the marketplace.

My waiting time, whether pondering the Scriptures through the Holy Spirit's empowerment or gazing upon him within, means saying no to all self-preferences and all means of human control. Waiting says, I am helpless *and can do nothing for myself.* Even receiving from him means he gives me what he wants me to have (Ps. 145:15–19) and I receive it with thanksgiving.

Paul said, "I die daily" (1 Cor. 15:31). Waiting is a way to turn from self-focus and self-love, dying to what our emotions and minds may be demanding. Waiting is an opening up to an invisible, but oh so real Person. He teaches us to behold him "But we all, with an open face beholding as in a glass the glory of the Lord, are changed into the same image from glory to glory even as by the Spirit of the Lord" (2 Cor. 3:18).

Will you begin to add five or ten minutes a day to be totally present to God, to give your undivided attention to him, following a tried and true pattern of great women and men of prayer from our past?

Waiting on God So He Can Teach Us

"My people are destroyed for lack of knowledge."

Hosea 4:6

Some years ago I was at my place of prayer and had been reading the spine-chilling account of Revelation 7:9–17, which pictures Jesus as Lord of all. All nations, kindreds, people, and tongues appear before him, worshiping him and singing praises to him.

This powerful biblical scene shall come to pass at some future time known only to God. As I read it that day I bowed low before him, worshiping him as my transcendent Lord of all! In a deep sense I entered into the worship and praise of our victorious, risen, and triumphant Lord of lords.

He is truly out beyond us. The scope of his kingship cannot be revealed by our external wisdom, but only through the indwelling Holy Spirit, who will from time to time pull back the curtain as we meditate in the Scriptures, enabling us to see more fully his divine lordship. Many of you have experienced the elevating expansion of seeing Jesus as Lord over all. The Holy Spirit reveals Jesus to us in ever-widening ways so we can begin to understand his stature and sonship.

As this humbling of myself before him in tremendous love and praise began to fade from my heart, I heard the Holy Spirit say something unexpected. "Margaret, you will actually bow before him one great day, but for now I don't want all your thoughts of Jesus to be external, outside of yourself. He is transcendent, but I want you to come to a deepening reality of Father, Son, and Holy Spirit *within* you at this present time."

The Remembrancer, the Holy Spirit, brought quickly to mind Jesus' words from John 14:17, "He dwelleth *with* you, and shall be *in* you" (emphasis added). John 14:21 adds, "He that hath my commandments, and keepeth them, he it is that loveth me: and he that loveth me shall be loved of my Father, and I will love him, and will *manifest myself to him*" (emphasis added). John 14:23 goes on to say, "If a man love me, he will keep my words: and my Father will love him, and *we will come unto him, and make our abode with him*" (emphasis added).

The Holy Spirit's words were so unexpected that I was taken aback. Other Scriptures began to flood my mind and spirit, such as "*we have this treasure in earthen vessels,* that the excellency of the power may be of God, and not of us" (2 Cor. 4:7, emphasis added). "*In him* we live, and move, and have our being" (Acts 17:28, emphasis added). "Christ *in* you, the hope of glory" (Col. 1:27, emphasis added). "I am crucified with Christ: nevertheless I live; yet not I, but *Christ liveth in me*" (Gal. 2:20, emphasis added).

The Word of God rose up in me with a new insight. He is within the believer! *Within me!* Living in my human spirit, never to leave, never to forsake, always present and alive unto me. God himself is alive in his people! I realized I had been too focused on God as being outside of me, and not enough on God within me.

Certainly we need to be aware of his glorious, external being out beyond all created things. But the wonder and miracle of Emmanuel, Jesus, is that he enters the human heart and lives also within, so we can commune together and companion each other (1 Cor. 6:17).

Now we are down to the core of what this book is about: how to get in touch with the Holy Spirit, who is our link with Jesus and the Father. We have been given a biblical pattern, a primary means of becoming God's friend. It is called waiting on God. This pattern goes back to the intimacy of the Trinity before the world was ever made, an interaction that included listening, waiting, and responding to one another (John 16:13–15; Acts 2:32–33). Waiting is the secret to life with God, as he lovingly trains us to know his voice (John 10), to enjoy his personhood (John 15:15), to receive his grace and mercy, and to respond to him as he meets our needs (1 John 3:1–2). As we wait on him, he teaches us how to be quiet, serene, responsive to his indwelling Spirit, both within us and through the quickening of his marvelous written Word, the Scriptures (Isa. 30:15).

In his wonderful book *Waiting on God* Andrew Murray defines it this way: "Waiting on God is a pool of listening, of being quiet, that surrounds prayer." Murray goes on to say that waiting is not prayer *per se* but allowing God to respond to us after we have prayed or talked to him.

There are no words from any language that I could borrow to speak of the joy and peace that have come to everyone I know, and to me, as we have lingered, waited, and listened in our secret places of prayer. We have not only talked to God but have allowed him to speak to us so we can have a conversation.

Waiting on God is the most urgently needed aspect in our devotional lives. Without waiting on God there can never be a mutual conversation.

God's Commitment

Such interconnectedness exists between what God does and what we are able to do as he constantly seeks to help us that there will always be an overlapping of our combined commitments. It is impossible to speak of one and not the other. Waiting on God means we take a much less aggressive role, a more subdued and reverent posture, creating the humble atmosphere necessary for him to be able to reveal himself in our spirit. Humanly speaking, our emotions and intellect are in such powerful dominance that even when we come to God we unknowingly prohibit him from being able to manifest himself within us. Our mental pride and self-sufficiency are so preeminent they cut off his expression. If he does begin to well up within us, we are too frantic and noisy to perceive him or are too afraid to allow him to be himself.

The prophet Elijah's behavior, as described in 1 Kings 19:11–13, substantiates what I am saying. Elijah was unable to hear God speak in his still, small voice until the great and strong wind that rent the rocks was past. "The Lord was not in the wind, the Lord was not in the earthquake, nor was God in the fire, but after the fire the still small voice."

1. He loves to reveal himself to us. Our God loves to come; he wants to come forth in us, to rise up in us in all his beauty. Only after we have waited long enough to get still, quiet, and able to perceive him, however, does he begin to minister to us as he yearns to minister. Any problems of his seeming not to come rest not on him but on us. A readiness to receive emerges as we remain steady during the opening, often unsettled period of time.

A young woman in our praying community recently experienced a life-changing encounter with Jesus. As we sat quietly together in the presence of the indwelling Jesus, he was able to pour out on her a tremendous, unconditional love that comforted her heart once she finally got calm and receptive so she could receive his love for her. Even her face looked different.

2. *He delights in meeting every need we have.* How he yearns to minister to us in whatever way we may need at the time! He will meet every earthly human need and every spiritual need in amazing ways if we can learn to cooperate with him (Isa. 49:10). He loves to love us; he longs to satisfy our needs for love so we can never return to our previous way of living (1 John 4:16). He loves to guide and direct us (Isa. 30:21). He loves to change our attitudes and dispositions (Eph. 4:24).

Any time given to God is multiplied many times over when it comes to his response to us. The great tragedy that we all encounter in our waiting experience is that many of our significant needs go unmet because we fail to grasp the significance of this time alone with him.

My mind turns to an older woman in our praying community, when I think of those persons who are walking radiantly in the midst of great tribulation. She is finding, as a result of her waiting on God, that she has available to her tremendous strength both physically and spiritually. Every day of her life is filled with great needs in both of these areas, and these needs are being met in the presence of Jesus through the Holy Spirit. She is a living miracle. My friend has found the empowerment of the Holy Spirit in the daily, long-term, lingering presence of God. Her needs are not something unique to her. We each have these needs, and the solution that she found is open to each of us as well.

I believe all the denominations have majored so strongly on the instantaneous works of grace—rebirth, baptism, the infilling of the Holy Spirit—that we have failed to teach the biblical pattern of waiting in his presence, not only daily but moment by moment! I fear we have made some of the great mysteries of the inner life too quick and easy to be in true alignment with the many biblical references to being cleansed and transformed into the image of Jesus. We simply do not spend enough time in his presence or in the Scriptures for the transforming to take place. The greatest art of all, relating to God, takes time and practice.

We can accept Jesus quickly, but having stepped inside the door does not constitute oneness with Jesus in all our character and personality. We need much time in his presence to be like him. Many feel only a few experiences in waiting on God are needed, but actually many experiences are necessary. He is determined, however, to cause the very life of Jesus to be the most vital aspect of our character. This will not happen without pain to our fleshly nature, which does not want to lay down its powerful need to control.

In the Word of God many Scriptures speak about waiting on God and about his active participation and commitment to us. Following are six of the best-known from the Old and New Testaments.

Old Testament

Psalm 130:5–6: I wait for the LORD, my soul doth wait, and in his word do I hope. My soul waiteth for the Lord more than they that watch for the morning: I say, more than they that watch for the morning.

Proverbs 8:34–35: Blessed is the man that heareth me, watching daily at my gates, waiting at the posts of my doors. For whoso findeth me findeth life, and shall obtain favour of the LORD.

Isaiah 40:28–31: Hast thou not known? Hast thou not heard, that the everlasting God, the Lord, the Creator of the ends of the earth, fainteth not, neither is weary? There is no searching of his understanding. He giveth power to the faint; and to them that have no might he increaseth strength. Even the youths shall faint and be weary, and the young men shall utterly fall: But they that wait upon the Lord shall renew their strength; they shall mount up with wings as eagles; they shall run, and not be weary; and they shall walk, and not faint.

New Testament

Matthew 11:28–30: Come unto me, all ye that labour and are heavy laden, and I will give you rest. Take my yoke upon you, and learn of me; for I am meek and lowly in heart: and ye shall find rest unto your souls. For my yoke is easy, and my burden is light.

Acts 13:2: As they ministered [waited] to the Lord, and fasted, the Holy Ghost said, Separate me Barnabas and Saul for the work whereunto I have called them.

2 Corinthians 3:18: But we all, with open face beholding as in a glass the glory of the Lord, are changed into the same image from glory to glory even as by the Spirit of the Lord.

By these Scriptures we see that he has extended a warm invitation to come to him. The promise of the Father is that he will always uphold his commitment to his children.

3. He deepens our capacity to receive more and more of him. The deeper our capacity to receive him, the more he is able to give. Only he can alter our capacity to receive as we learn to wait in more openness, day by day. There is no shortcut to maturity in waiting; it comes "little by little" (Exod. 23:30). He causes us to relax within and we become more comfortable with him as we go along. He commits to being activated in us as we linger in his presence. Zechariah 2:13 says, "Be silent, O all flesh, before the LORD: for he is raised up out of his holy habitation." This Scripture promises his rising up within us. He trains us to know him ever more intimately and to receive his workings within us without fear and insecurity. Our cooperation with him, by giving him "our undivided, loving attention," as the great saints say, is the type of yieldedness that allows him more dominion within. Love for him grows within our hearts so that we love to look upon him and look forward eagerly to our time together.

Let me offer two closing thoughts about his full commitment to us. First, I realize we will be purified when we see him (1 John 3:2), but Scripture does teach we are to be cleansed from all filthiness of flesh and spirit (2 Cor. 7:1). Much of this inner cleansing comes as our lifestyle is altered so we truly humble ourselves before God and learn to wait on him.

"There is a Divine Person—let us bow our heads and worship Him—the Holy Spirit who proceeds from the Father, and He it is who renews us in the spirit of our minds," wrote Charles Spurgeon. "When one believes in Jesus, the Spirit enters into the heart, creating within it a new life; that life struggles and contends against the old life, or rather the old death, and as it struggles it gathers strength and grows; it masters the evil, and puts its foot upon the neck of the tendency to sin. Do you feel this Spirit within you? You must be under its power or perish. If any man have not the Spirit of Christ he is none of His. I would not have you imagine that in death everything is to be accomplished for us mysteriously in the last solemn article; we are to look for a work of grace in life, a present work, molding our characters among men."[5]

Second, the forgotten message of today is the reciprocal friendship that is possible as we cultivate a daily time in his written Word and learn to gaze upon the incarnational Word of God (2 Cor. 3:18).

Our Commitment

God is eager to help us. "No man can come to me, except the Father which hath sent me draw him" (John 6:44). His grace and his love are responsible for all of our actions toward him. At our slightest movement in his direction, he is fully prepared. He runs to meet us in unconditional love and grace. There is no one like Jesus! He is on the constant lookout for any feeble response on our part. He more than overarches our lives with his wondrous love. There is no searching out his love for us. What is our commitment?

1. We need to reverence and honor the Godhead by taking a lowly place. We are prone to think if God were a human being, flesh and blood, it would be easier to communicate with him. But even if he were flesh as Jesus once was, we would still have to do this relationship his way. Our aggressive, assertive, carnal flesh, our larger-than-life egos, and our personalities would still have to yield, to be humble and quiet before him, to let him deal with us. Learning the depth of submissiveness and surrender necessary in our daily time with God is the issue. The language of meekness and lowliness is a foreign language today, but it is still Jesus' way. Barriers and resistance to God go deep within each one of us. Only in learning to surrender as the Holy Spirit guides us within the context of our time together brings these barriers down.

2. We need to lay down our control so he can be the initiator. Waiting on God will be the hardest thing you have ever done, but it will also be the most thrilling. Why is waiting on God so difficult? Because we do not know how not to be in complete control. We live in a society in which we no longer have to wait for anything, in which we have everything available to us almost instantly. This instantaneous lifestyle has deprived us of some of the value of waiting, such as appreciating all that goes into making events happen, reliance on others, and getting in touch with ourselves. Our own self-reliance and self-effort are so pronounced we carry them with us into everything we do and say and they go into high gear every time we seek to draw near to him. We somehow feel it is up to us to produce this daily fellowship with God.

But it is not up to us. Our part is to receive humbly whatever movement toward us he wants to make. Have you ever been so hungry in the middle of the afternoon that you went to a vending machine or a fast-food stand and practically inhaled something to satisfy your hunger? When you did, did you remember that a good meal would be waiting for you in about an hour? When we take control and eat at the body's first sign of hunger, we miss the truly satisfying comfort that comes with a regular meal. The snack spoils our desire for the real food that will nurture our bodies.

The way the snack spoils a meal is the same way our control and our worldly desire for instant gratification spoil our time at the heavenly banquet table (Ps. 106:13). The power of the daily hour with God is that we begin to learn not to take over; instead we ask the Holy Spirit to be the one in charge. "Holy Spirit, how can I get out of your way? What do you want me to do in this time with you? Do you want me to open the Scriptures and read? To look upon Jesus?" A young woman I know told me recently that she tells the Holy Spirit, "I hand the clipboard to you and lay down my agenda!"

What a shock to our insatiable drive for control, even in our waiting, to find that what we evaluate as our poorest waiting experience, which is often cluttered with distracted concentration or restlessness in our soul and spirit, is actually helpful because we are *not* in control. Our poverty and inadequacy surface during these times and we see ourselves as we really are. As painful as it might be, such a time is actually a good time of waiting, because as we cry out to God he comes to us. "In our weakness he is strong" (2 Cor. 12:9–10).

Paul said, "Lord what would You have me do?" (Acts 9:6). Paul had been in control, and God had to knock him off his feet, push his face in the dust, and bring him down so he would say, "I will do what you want me to do!"

Jesus could do nothing in Paul until he was brought low and kept low, alone, blind, with no food, praying for three days until help came. Then the Holy Spirit taught him for years in the desert (Gal. 1:17–18). Paul's self-assertion and carnal determination were too strong for God to have room to work; Paul waited on God for years before his ministry really began.

You lead and I will follow: That was the essence of Paul's surrender, and it should be ours as well. Our daily hour is our time to let God lead while we follow. Over and over in our time with God we will need to lay down what we think, what we feel we should do. We must allow the Holy Spirit to come forward and be Lord over us and Lord over the hour. He is in charge and must be allowed to express that control as he sees fit. Only one person can be in control, and that person must be God! How can he be Lord of our lives if we will not let him take complete control of our daily time together?

"But Margaret," you gasp, "that's frightening. What if nothing happens?"

It would be better for "nothing" to happen than for you or me to jump in and try to make it happen. If we continue to take control, God will allow us to be in control, but it will not be the Holy Spirit stirring in our hearts.

Remember, we are not speaking of the emotional realm but of the Holy Spirit taking action in our human spirit. Whenever we try to force God to do something by using our emotions or minds, God is not at work—we are. I truly believe that if we will allow him to lead the best we know how, he will lead us into ever-widening experiences of release, surrender, cleansing of our basic fear of him, and cleansing of our fear of ourselves. Without a time set apart to let him be Lord, our ability to relate to him does not mature but remains as it was when we first met him. The growing depth of surrender he desires comes as we gaze upon his face, with increasing love flowing from years of knowing him.

3. We need to realize that our self-focus will make waiting on God more difficult. Another handicap to waiting on God is our absorption with ourselves, our families, our towns, and our churches, forgetting Jesus' great concern for all. Only as we begin to look on Jesus in daily meditation can his love and presence break into the force of our self-preoccupation. Even the poorest waiting, in distraction and listlessness, but waiting on God, will allow the blessed Holy Spirit to begin to shift our focus from us to him! He will draw us more and more into looking at him, not ourselves, if we will persist daily.

4. We must lay down our perfectionism and need for performance. I started waiting on God years ago with high hopes of doing it perfectly. Needless to say, that hope was quickly squashed. I waited on him so poorly, in fact, that I failed more than I succeeded. But he has helped me to keep on keeping on. I am available to him, though powerless. He seems to like the persistence that only he can give, because no matter how inadequate the time is by my evaluation, he keeps moving toward me. How I love him for his continual faithfulness! The more helpless and hopeless I have been, understanding the truth of my condition has caused me to submit all the more. I know I cannot wait on God adequately in my own power, but there are times when I still try! My time with God does not depend on me, but on him. If I show up, yielded, quiet, and open toward him as our friendship deepens, he will reveal himself more and more. On hundreds of occasions I have left my prayer place feeling that, by my standards, I had wasted my time and had absolutely nothing to show for it. Imagine my surprise as I walk to the kitchen, having failed again to focus as I should or could, to hear him speak to me in unbelievably loving tones.

I was unloading the dishwasher one day after what I thought was a futile time of waiting when suddenly I heard him say, "You've got forty-five minutes. Let's drive out in the country before you begin counseling."

His spontaneity is so delightful. "Jesus, is it okay to do that?" I asked.

"Sure, let's go."

That thirty-minute drive will always be in my heart. It occurred when I was in deep need and stress and when I would not have thought to use my time in that way. The afternoon was a joy because he was so near, so lovingly thoughtful of me. His presence was real and sweetly comforting.

He is always there, and he does and will respond. Time with him trains us to be in touch with him all through the day. There is great power in coming daily: "Draw nigh to God, and he will draw nigh to you" (James 4:8; Exod. 16:4, 13–15).

When we first begin to open our lives to the Holy Spirit and his ministry within us, we will often wrestle with him. Our self-will is so strong. We are used to doing things our way, and the flesh will refuse to wait. If you find you cannot sit quietly and wait, ask the Holy Spirit to help you get into the Scriptures. Sometimes in the beginning or during certain periods of stress we cannot avoid cutting short our time of waiting, but meditating on his Word, aided by the Holy Spirit, keeps us in the presence of God where he can minister to us. Remember, however, that it is easy to "hide out" by reading Scripture, and not spend time waiting.

Two closing thoughts: First, there are many people, precious to the Father, who have mental health problems. This book on the inner ministry of the Holy Spirit is for persons with a reasonable amount of emotional wholeness, persons able to function as rational human beings.

Second, allowing the indwelling Holy Spirit to be alive in us has nothing to do with New Age meditation or Eastern thought. We are speaking of the biblical promise of the Father, the Holy Spirit, entering the heart of the believer and, through the biblical practice of waiting on him, being given the supreme place in our lives as Lord and Master.

Acts 13:1–4 records that as the church at Antioch waited and ministered to the Father, the Holy Spirit spoke and guided them. The Spirit is still available today to Christians if we will wait on him. As Andrew Murray wrote, "Learn to say of every want and every failure and every lack of needful grace: I have waited too little upon God, or He would have given me in due season all I needed."[6]

Responsibility Belongs to the Holy Spirit

Waiting on God is an acting out of a ritual of dependency on God.

Margaret Therkelsen

As we come to our waiting time every day, we bring into God's presence a diversity of human experiences. He begins to teach us that we can bring all our life experiences to him, no matter how big or small, how painful or how joyful, how humdrum or monotonous.

When I first started waiting on God, I was hesitant to bring some situations to him because I was ashamed of my conduct. I was like a little girl who only wants to tell her parents what she feels is safe to tell them. At other times I was unaware of attitudes within that were preventing him from working. But as he enabled me to persist and as his presence began to manifest within my spirit, I began to look forward eagerly to sitting with him, because I saw I could bring any and all circumstances into his presence. The best thing I could do in all situations, in fact, was to stop running and doing and go to him (Isa. 55:1–3).

The indwelling Holy Spirit is far more faithful than we give him credit for being. He delights in anyone who will fling wide the doors of his or her being to him. He begins to "work in [us] both to will and to do of his good pleasure" (Phil. 2:1–13). He changes our human wills, as we let him empty us out of self daily. We begin to will what he wills and to do what he wants done. We are unaware of this inner working at first, but as we fellowship day after day, he surfaces new desires and longings in our hearts. Our passion begins to be for him to have his way in everything.

At one point I was giving an hour daily to my devotional life, along with as much extra time as I could spend, particularly on weekends. But he was working in me a yearning so wistful, so sweet, to be more and more with him, waiting, sitting at his feet. Nothing else appealed to me as he did, and I began to long for more time with him.

He showed me that my experience of him was more precious than anything or anyone. I was teaching piano in a fine arts college and loving it, but my daily schedule prevented more than a couple of hours a day with him, and that was stretched tightly. A thought began to waft across my heart in quiet moments as I waited: "Do you love me enough to lay down all your training, your years of teaching, your love of the instrument, to leave music behind and spend more time with me?"

It was a daring thought, and one I never imagined I would have to face, yet it struck a chord of great joy within me. He was opening up to me a new way of life, even as he had empowered me to open up to him. He loves to guide us in just such a way, first opening up the inner person to more of him, then letting what we find there begin to pour out in life calling and work.

As I waited on God about this as well as other issues, fear often rose up in me that I should not and could not do as he seemed to be suggesting. Other days I felt it was right.

I remember one morning in particular. I felt a desperate reaching out for God. I simply had to hear from him as to exactly what he wanted me to do; my whole future was hanging in the balance. He had to tell me today; I needed to hear exactly how it would all take place. I felt confident this was the day on which the decision would be made.

There are times in the life of prayer when desperation helps us crash through the barriers and obstacles that separate us from God. We simply will not take no for an answer, or accept his silence for his presence rather than his absence, as I had been taught! We persist until the shadows flee away and we get to him. My mother did not put much stock in the "dark night of the soul." She felt the Holy Spirit was given as our Helper to dispel darkness and teach us to know experientially that he is always present to us. She believed that if we persist we can break through to him. I believe this also; on many occasions he has enabled me to persist until things are clear between us.

On this occasion, however, my desperation veiled some inner attitudes that made it hard for me to come into his presence. At the base of these attitudes was a restlessness, containing some anger. The anger told me I had fallen into an old trap of feeling that he had demanded too much from me. All my inadequacies and all my insecurities surfaced in the face of changing careers. This fork in the road of my life journey was causing me to be dependent on him to guide me in ways I had never allowed before. When challenged to this depth, anger toward him rose up as I felt I could not meet his standard. I also felt that waiting on God was too sobering; facing my sin and self was not exactly fun. Impatience, a terrible failing of mine, was in white heat that morning.

The Scriptures are full of examples of people crying out to God. Even my desperation was a crying out, and my heart and soul cried out, "Holy Spirit, come, help me, teach me your way." I knew it would be hard to get to him when I felt so driven for an answer about my future; I was too agitated and too demanding. All I could do was pour out my feelings—all of them—to him (Ps. 62:1–8).

Even as I wrestled with how I felt, the Holy Spirit began to help me see that the first thing I needed was to be saved from myself. I needed to set aside my intensity and urgency to know God's will. Striving and straining out of human desire, in human strength, were getting in the way of getting quiet before him. I had taken over again.

My needs were so great that they, not God, filled my consciousness. When my needs soared that large over my vision of him, my soulish realm kicked in. Fearful anxiety and insecurity flooded over me, and of course Satan was right there to say, "You can't really get to the Father. You wouldn't dare be such a fool as to get out of music. What are you thinking? What could you do? You can't pray all the time."

But even as Satan taunted me, the Holy Spirit gently reminded me deep in my spirit, "I am responsible for your spiritual life! I am responsible for your human life, including your profession. You can't bring this about and will never be able to do it yourself. All you need to do is present yourself to me and allow me to teach you how to be nothing, assuming no responsibility except to be helpless and dependent on me. Wait on me. Desire to let me do it all (1 Peter 5:7–11). Submit to my timetable, my plan, my provision beginning now. This is my call. Rest in me; trust me to work it out."

As he spoke lovingly, correcting me, my frustration began to die down. My soulish emotions came to rest and relief. The drivenness of trying to force God into action because of my great need fell away. The strength of my self-will was brought low and I saw it for the terrible sin it is. "Lord," I prayed, "forgive me. I repent. I willingly put my flesh under. Through the power of the cross I ask you to mortify my flesh under the precious blood of Jesus. I don't need an answer to my dilemma today. I just need to decrease so you can increase! I don't want to keep getting in your way."

It was as if the dear Holy Spirit, deep in my soul and spirit, was putting out the fires of self-drivenness, pulling back that part of me that even thought it could force God's hand. The longing for Jesus now was full of faith, not fear. He empowered me to persist in waiting, to have faith that indeed he had come and he was to be trusted.

"Lord, I wait on you. I'm here because I love you. There is no place I would rather be. I do see my sin of trying to force you to answer me in my way; I praise you for showing me and forgiving me." I took a deep breath and relaxed. I did not have to do anything but be in his presence. When he took me on, he took on all my burdens and cares, every decision, every venture. He would show me the way (Ps. 40:1–3; Isa. 45:2–3).

We sat quietly, and the Remembrancer began to remind me of the Scripture, "Take unto you the whole armor of God . . . and having done all, to stand" (Eph. 6:13). He showed me how I must stand against giving up in my waiting; stand against Satan's pestering, as my emotions roll fiercely over me; resist abandoning the holy place of waiting until his presence begins to illumine my darkness, "and in [his] light, we . . . see light" (Ps. 36:9). "Unto the upright there ariseth light in the darkness" (Ps. 112:4).

I heard the clock chime in the hallway; my encounter with him had taken more than an hour. I had completely forgotten time—he was so real and so dear! Oh, how sweet the presence of Jesus! There is no one like him! In his presence my needs were dwarfed to nothing, because he showed himself strong within me, weak and pitiful as I am! The excellency of the power was his, not mine! The arising of the Holy Spirit in me was quickening a freshness of my faith in him. There was peace deep down in my spirit, and my soul was under his control. He had calmed my fears, helped me to persist against the pull of the enemy on my weaknesses, and brought me into a safe place of resting in him.

I thought it was all over, but one of the most beautiful and engaging traits of the Holy Spirit is his spontaneity. He is always full of surprises when we wait on him. Just to be with him, in close harmony and oneness, was all I needed. I knew particular answers would come as they were needed. I just needed him, for out of being with him come the answers to every need (Matt. 6:33).

A sense of well-being and of being lovingly cared for rose up in me. Emotionally I felt nothing, but his presence in my spirit brought the peace only he can bring.

"Stay with me; don't hurry away," he said. So we sat together. I had forgotten about myself in the joy of his presence. How healing it was, how full of relief and freedom, to forget oneself and be centered in him.

"My thoughts are not your thoughts, neither are your ways my ways," came from deep within me (Isa. 55:8).

"Lord, I see."

Softly yet powerfully, out of that peace that passes understanding, he began to bring to mind persons for me to pray over. Some I had not seen for years, some I had seen last week. There was concern, yet ease, in lifting up one after another as they came. This went on for twenty to thirty minutes. To pray for others was not on my mind when I started my waiting. I was focused only on what I needed.

Not only had he turned me from myself, but we concluded that time of waiting, as he wanted, in self-forgetful intercession for others. When we wait, we do not order his conduct, though I had found myself, out of too much focus on my own need, trying to do that very thing. The awesome and wonderful experience of waiting is to see him afresh and anew, to be lifted out of ourselves and be vessels for his Holy Spirit to fulfill whatever he desires. Often it will be his prayer ministry. But the wonder of waiting on God is that though I am my worst enemy and you are your worst enemy, the Holy Spirit will bring forth his ministry to us and through us as we wait.

Waiting is not easy, and probably never will be. To be brought to any self-forgetfulness is to allow him dominion within. It involves much processing, much inward failure, as he teaches us how to relinquish what we feel and think. Only he can bring us to inner resolution as we persist in waiting.

I did not get a clear-cut yea or nay that day. I did, however, receive from him something far more needed: his presence surging up in my spirit, and in his presence, contentment and love. I knew that when he was ready he would guide in the area of my profession. And he did unfold it all. He was teaching me to trust him lovingly and forget about my needs and plans.

As I basked in his loving presence all my needs were met. I had needed him and his reassurance of love more than his answer to the question, What shall I do?

He is always more important than our problems and needs. That day he poured out himself on me so powerfully that my faith and expectancy that he would guide were reaffirmed. I left the place of waiting light as a feather. My faith was strong. My plans were still fuzzy, but I was at peace because he rose up in me as the Mighty One.

The soulish realm gets us all flustered, but he himself is our peace (Eph. 2:14). In the fullness of time, at the appointed hour, he moves in all the details we need. Until then, his very presence empowers us to trust, obey, and love (Heb. 10:35–38).

God's Commitment

In one sense, his commitment to us is finished. He has done for us all he can do. "For Christ is . . . entered . . . into heaven itself, now to appear in the presence of God for us" (Heb. 9:24). Waiting on him does not bring him closer to us because he is *within* us: "What, know ye not that your body is the temple of the Holy Spirit, which is in you" (1 Cor. 6:19). He cannot be any more present or real than he is. Rather, waiting brings us closer to him. The difficulty lies in the fact that our ability to perceive him is limited because we are dulled by "the lust of the flesh, and the lust of the eyes, and the pride of life" (1 John 2:15–17).

As we wait we turn toward him, "with open face beholding as in a glass the glory of the Lord" (2 Cor. 3:18). He will begin to manifest his presence in many ways in our spirits. In the following pages I lift up for you what seem to be the most recurring and representative aspects of him that I have seen in my life. I hasten to say that there are many ways of his coming that I have not yet experienced.

1. He will open to us the floodgates of his love. The sudden, spontaneous welling up within our spirit of the Holy Spirit in God's great love for us is the most powerful of all his manifestations. With no doubts whatsoever, we will know we are loved and precious to him. The Holy Spirit is the love of God, shedding abroad his love in our hearts. He will make that love real as we wait (Rom. 5:5).

Many times his love will wash over our emotions, but just as often our emotions will not be stimulated. Still, we will be freshly encouraged, lifted up, reminded that he does indeed love us. We will be strengthened by the reality that he is within. As this love is awakened within we will sense the love of the Father, Son, and Holy Spirit. This repeated opening of the floodgates of his love for us is the single most defining sign of the Holy Spirit's life within. Ephesians 3:16–19 speaks of the ministry of the Holy Spirit in the inner man, the tremendous strengthening with the might of the Holy Spirit as he reveals more and more of God's eternal heavenly love until our roots are grounded in that love. Those roots clinging to the foundation of God's nature of love cause us to be fixed and immovable, regardless of Satan's tactics.

I believe that as we wait daily he begins to manifest his power within to expand our capacity to experience his love deeply, to be able to receive more of that love, even as he gains more access into our brokenness and woundedness. His yearning to bring dimensions of his love to all our inner person is part and parcel of who he is. Probably the most distinguishing mark of people who become more intimate with the Holy Spirit is the amazing opening up of their beings to the heights, depths, lengths, and breadths of God's amazing love. They continually flow into the mighty love of God, which goes beyond any other experience possible to man. His love certainly cannot be reached through contact with other humans. His love comes through contact with him and him alone. To be freed up from oneself, to move out into the soundless depths of the oceans of God's love is an ongoing movement of God's life within his children that comes as we allow him freedom in our inner world, as we wait on him.

I know of no other way for our shallow, self-centered human love to be released from its murky boundaries into the fullness of God's unselfish love than daily to give God an open door into our tainted love as we wait for him to come. Human love then begins to give way to the divine in worship, in purging, and in repeated immersions into divine love. I know of no other way to express this concept adequately; I only know that those who wait do experience it. The Holy Spirit brings us to a deep commitment to obey the love commandments of Jesus (John 13:34–35; 15:10, 12, 17). When it is hard to love, we no longer cry out, "I won't love," but the Holy Spirit loves through us (1 John 4:7–13).

After speaking of the wondrous gifts of the Holy Spirit in 1 Corinthians chapter 12, Paul sweeps into 1 Corinthians chapter 13, saying, "Let me share something even more glorious; let me share God's very character of divine love, his very nature of selfless love. This is the more excellent way to experience him loving all parts of ourselves and then to allow him to love through us with his pure, holy love." Surely earth's highest experience is to allow the Holy Spirit enough time to teach us more and more of his love, to be lifted out of conditional, demanding, self-seeking human love and into God's life of love flowing in us and through us. This is what he wants for every one of his children.

This is the promise of the Father, God's indwelling Holy Spirit of love. He has not just been given permission to enter and take up his residency within, but he is free to open up the dimensions of his love about which we know nothing.

We desperately need to experience his love in every area of our living. Most of us spend more time in front of the television or involved in any number of activities than we spend in front of Jesus. If we would take those hours and begin to wait on him, he would save not only our souls but also our nation.

Why? Because his love alone alters us, transforms us, cleanses us. As we open our natures to this redemptive and eternal love, the very quintessence of Calvary love, he will stir up the gift of God within us, the Holy Spirit, the unspeakable love of God (2 Tim. 1:6–7).

As full of ourselves as we are, it is not easy to look upon Jesus and let him redeem us from ourselves. But what a privilege to draw water out of the wells of salvation (Isa. 12:3). Jesus said, "If any man thirst, let him come to me, and drink. . . . [and] out of his belly [innermost being] shall flow rivers of living water" (John 7:37–39).

John 7:39 tells us that when Jesus spoke these words, "the Holy Spirit was not yet given; because that Jesus was not yet glorified." Now the Holy Spirit has been given to lead us into the riches and wonders of God's holy love. Are you daily being ministered to by the Holy Spirit in your inner person? His ministry to us is the healing, the cleansing, the restoring of the very life of God, who is love. The divine nature of love is imputed to us in our hearts, let loose in our hearts, to cause us to enter as fully as possible into him, that we might live *through* him (1 John 4:7–9). To live in and through him all our living must go through his very nature of love, be purified of self, and flow out into more and more of him and his love nature. This can be accomplished in no other way than in time with God, where he begins a deep cleansing of our inner natures. Spending time, giving him our undivided attention, and crying out for more of him allow him to do within what he wants to do (Gal. 5:22–25)!

My heart goes out to Christians who, after years of knowing Jesus, remain in the same depth of love as when they first met him. They have missed the daily cleansing and mingling of heart to heart with him. Their level of loving him and others is not altered either, because they have not understood the Holy Spirit and his inner ministry to the believer. He is capable, if given opportunity, of swelling his love nature to new dimensions of appropriation within us.

The purpose of all our time with God is to be vitally engaged in a progressive way in his very life and nature, to be drawn steadily, surely, into more of his kind of love and drawn out of our human kind of love (Rom. 8:35–39).

He is bigger than all life as we know it. His love is all in all, and he loves to reveal himself as a real live Being, with facets of his love nature and character opening up daily as we wait. As we learn not to run from him he begins to minister to us, pouring out his love on us. Oswald Chambers writes, "The great need is to receive the Holy Spirit, that he may do *in* us all that Jesus Christ did *for* us on the cross."[7]

2. He will invade our inner lives with the reality of Jesus' presence. As his love nature begins to rise up within, a strong reality of Jesus' presence will invade and pervade our inner lives. The Holy Spirit reveals Jesus (John 16:12–15). When we are born again, we meet him and love him, but he is so far beyond our comprehension, and we are so bound up in ourselves. He yearns for a daily sharing of our lives together, knowing it takes time. Only in his presence of love do we feel safe enough to allow him to disclose himself, but my perception is that he must be able to trust us enough to risk disclosing himself to us!

We need an ever-increasing vision and reality of Jesus and in Jesus. Our praying community loves to read the Gospels and reflect upon Jesus, his life, what he said and did. God yearns for us to have a nurturing experience of Jesus that only comes as the Holy Spirit reveals Jesus to us. This will go on for all eternity (Eph. 2:4–10). We should never leave our place of waiting on God until the Holy Spirit has drawn us into deeper waters of God's love and given us a fresh look at Jesus. Only the Holy Spirit, over the months and years as we look upon Jesus' face, can cause us to love him with all our heart, with all our soul, and with all our mind (Matt. 22:35–40; 2 Cor. 4:6).

3. He will give us his peace. As we wait on God we will sense a peace that passes all understanding and misunderstanding welling up from within us where he lives. Jesus says in John 14:27, "Peace I leave with you, my peace I give unto you: not as the world giveth, give I unto you. Let not your heart be troubled, neither let it be afraid." As the Holy Spirit releases the floodgates of God's love within and reveals to us the wonder of Jesus Christ, we find a powerful peace, a serenity, a confidence so rich that our fears and troubles vanish away in his light! Psalm 27:14 says, "He shall strengthen thine heart." As we are immersed in him, our human spirit is strengthened to be able to trust him. This untroubled trust emerges because we see him as he is.

4. He will give us insight and understanding. Deep in our hearts, as we bow in his presence, his wisdom begins to flood our thought processes. He illumines insight and understanding. Suddenly the light goes on and we say, "Aha!" We perceive the truth through Jesus, who is the Way, the Truth, and the Life, whereas moments before we failed to see. The dear Holy Spirit has given insight and understanding, as Isaiah 11:1–3 says. As our minds become more stayed and fixed on him, we are able to keep the vision of him longer and he cleanses our thinking. He wants us to have perfect (or mature) peace because we are fixed in mind, emotions, and spirit to look upon him, no matter what is happening around us (Isa. 26:3).

5. Out of his presence he begins to guide and direct us. The guidance may come through mental impressions or new thoughts, often so simple and everyday in scope that we have failed to see the solutions we need! As we progress, we will hear him speak in our spirit, and his leading will be confirmed by his precious written Word and through other people.

Many times when we wait we will hear nothing; the account I wrote of in the beginning of this chapter is a case in point. But often we are not ready to perceive an answer anyway because we are too driven and full of self-importance. We must get to him and let him calm us down so we can hear his guidance and direction.

He loves to guide; in fact, I believe guiding is one of God's favorite pastimes. But he must train us to hear, and this training comes as we wait and listen, *daily,* reaching out to our indwelling Holy Spirit and letting him be our guide (Isa. 64:4).

6. When we have learned to linger in his presence, the prayer life of the Holy Spirit will begin to flow through us. He guides us into forgetting about ourselves (ah, what bliss), and he often begins to pray through us what is in the heart of God at that very moment. Sometimes names and situations will come, and we can join with the Holy Spirit to lift them into God's presence in Jesus' name. Sometimes the groanings and yearnings go so deep we find no words, and neither does the Holy Spirit, just yearnings too profound, beyond any vocabulary that will flow from our spirit. Let him have his way. He is the Helper and he is the Intercessor. He alone knows God's will (1 Cor. 2:7–16). Let these divine yearnings flow until they cease welling up within. They are the Holy Spirit's prayers. Often that yearning of the indwelling Spirit will go on not only for a day but days at a time. What a profound experience to be a vessel for the life of the Holy Spirit as he prays within us (Rom. 8:26–27).

7. In his manifest presence, we will find we fear him less. One of the deepest barriers is our fear of him. As we wait daily in his Word, however, and quietly open our life to him, he begins to reveal himself gradually as we are able to receive him (Mark 8:22–25). As we find our fear level going down and our expectancy or faith level going up, we will not want to cut short being with him. It is impossible to trust fully anyone we do not know and are afraid of as well. He yearns to teach us how to enjoy him, how to relate to him, how to experience him, but it takes openness on our part and time given over to him (Exod. 33; 1 John 4:18–19).

As our spiritual eyes are opened more and more to God, he cleanses our distorted perceptions of him. Then we begin to understand his nature more clearly.

As the promise of the Father, the Holy Spirit, fulfills his commitment to us, our relationship becomes so precious that to be aware of him is life itself, and to be unaware of him is death. We yearn for his companionship all through the day and he teaches us in our human spirit to stay close to him all day. To live with him and in him, with no separation, is our goal (Ps. 27:4; 89:14–16). We know our biggest need is to be so focused on him that we think of ourselves less and less. The most powerful form of self-denial is loving him so much that we forget ourselves (Heb. 11:27).

Just think! God Almighty wants such intimacy with us that he will live inside us, yearning for our attention and permission to be the dominant life within our life! That we could ever live so close to God is unbelievable. The Holy Spirit has been given to us for the very sake of that intimacy.

Our Commitment

The motley crew of followers Jesus worked with before he was taken to heaven were men who felt they could do anything Jesus wanted them to do. They were strong, self-reliant, experienced in the world's ways and (they thought) perfectly capable of standing on their own two feet. Peter said with great bravado, "Lord, I will never deny you!" He was cocky and sure of himself, and God had to let him crash as he relied on his own strength and selfhood. "I will lay down my life for thy sake," Peter said (John 13:37). But when he heard the cock crow the third time, it swept over him that nothing within himself was strong enough to keep him true to Jesus. He went out and wept like a baby (Matt. 26:75). He saw his need for self-glory, his self-expression, and in despair he cried like he had never cried in his life.

Peter's failure was inevitable because he was dependent on himself instead of Jesus, and he had not received the Holy Spirit's empowerment to be obedient. There is so much about ourselves we do not see, and until we come to the end of our human pride and energy, there is not much we can receive from God. I want to say again we must be brought again and again, day by day, to bankruptcy as we wait on God. We do not know the intensity of the power of our flesh to usurp the Holy Spirit's place. This carnal nature, which is full of pride and self-righteousness, is truly enmity against God. Only the Holy Spirit can deal with it (Rom. 8:5–8).

Waiting on God goes against the grain of our self-sufficiency and self-absorption. As we begin seriously and intentionally to wait from five to ten minutes daily, we begin to realize to a deeper degree the force of our fleshly, carnal soulish realm.

That domain of the soul is fortresslike and is so evident in our will to go our own way. It comes through the strength of personality, aggressive whether we are introverts or extroverts. The soul realm has great abilities and skills, is highly educated in survival tactics, and, down underneath, rules with an iron hand.

Our soulish realm does not like to be set aside for waiting on God, interacting with the Holy Spirit within by prayer, and listening to what God has to say about what we have prayed. It will rise in amazing strength when we sit down to look away from self and at Jesus (Gal. 5:16–18).

I have pondered much about the days of waiting on God recorded in the Book of Acts. The disciples did not even know what or whom they were waiting on. Yes, they knew

Jesus had said, "Ye shall receive power, after that the Holy Spirit is come upon you" (Acts 1:8), but no one, except Jesus and a few men and women in the Old Testament, had ever experienced the Holy Spirit. What did Jesus mean? What would the Holy Spirit be like? It is hard to imagine the unimaginable, particularly when God is involved! The disciples needed ten days to tarry in the upper room. They had known only human soulish power, and they had seen it put Jesus to death. But human power had failed to hold them steady: "They all forsook him, and fled" (Mark 14:50).

The disciples needed to be "emptied out" of their ideas, concepts, sins, and offenses against God and each other. They needed time to realize their self-glorification, their self-motivation in wanting Jesus to set up the kingdom their way. How important they had been, even when he came in his resurrected presence and tried to tell them to tarry until a whole new order of being was given them through the Holy Spirit. They asked him, then, about whether this was the time he would restore again the kingdom to Israel! They had absolutely no understanding because they had not yet been given the Holy Spirit (Acts 1:5–7). They needed to make restitution among themselves for trying to push ahead of one another in self-importance. They needed to be emptied of all personal need for recognition, all self-glory and self-bias, until their pride was brought low and they could only cling to the Holy Spirit.

It took God time to bring them to such humility. It takes him time to help us see that if he does not do the work, the work will not be done now or ever. It will take God much time daily with us as well, for we are cut from the same piece of fallen humanity as the early disciples.

Before Pentecost the disciples felt they could do what needed to be done better than anything God could do. After Pentecost they gladly shut the door to moving out on their own and moved only as he guided. In a deep sense we enter into an "Upper Room" kind of waiting each time we wait to be lifted by the Holy Spirit into a realm of God's activity rather than human activity. In other words, our daily waiting for his life to be manifest is like a miniature pre-Pentecost, and then he comes as he wills in our daily Pentecost.

For the disciples, the waiting certainly was not easy. They wanted to rush right out and get the church birthed, but they knew they could not! They waited for the Holy Spirit's movement in them. You and I must wait also for the life of the Holy Spirit to move in us.

In Galatians 6:7–17 Paul says, "If you live out of your flesh, rather than out of the Holy Spirit within you, you will reap corruption. I glory in the cross of Jesus, by whom the world is crucified unto me and I unto the world." John says it another way: "I say no to the love of the world, the lust of the flesh, the lust of the eye, the pride of life" (1 John 2:15–16). In other words, we must be dead to the world system of acting in our own energy out of our own understanding. The Holy Spirit's wisdom, love, and power is all that will be necessary. My soul realm, my selfhood, dies or gives up its position to the life of the Holy Spirit. I take the cross by saying no to my self-preservation and self-pity so that God's will, which is what the Holy Spirit wants, can be accomplished. I love this quote from Watchman Nee, "The greatest temptation for an earnest and zealous saint is to engage his own strength in God's service rather than to wait humbly for the Holy Spirit to will and to perform."[8]

Waiting on God affords the time, the quiet, and the setting to say, "Holy Spirit, right now I deny self. I take up my cross of saying no to all I want, and I would follow Jesus in coming apart to allow you to be with me and I with you. I give you permission to illumine and correct me of my soulish need for self-glory. I ask you to take the spirit of the world out of me, to cleanse me of all religious spirits. I ask you to transform me into being like Jesus inside and out." Then I give him the time he needs to manifest that transformation.

As we say no to our soul realm, empowered by his life emerging stronger and stronger in us as we wait, he helps us die to self more and more so the Holy Spirit is released to be the activity, the purpose, and the rule of our lives. John 3:30 says it so well, "He must increase, but I must decrease."

I believe a daily, even moment by moment, life of dependency on the Holy Spirit begins in us as we wait for him to rise up within and take the headship to which he is entitled. A level of authority and power is released in and through those who really open their lives to him in deep humility through waiting. That authority and power is the manifest life of Jesus, the Holy Spirit indwelling the believer (2 Cor. 3:3–9). The second chapter of Philippians speaks of God causing Jesus to be brought to the lowest place, which was death on the cross (v. 8). Out of that death, the Holy Spirit was brought forth. The saints of the ages have taught that only from Calvary, in a death to self, comes the resurrection life of God the Holy Spirit. This was Jesus' pattern and it must be ours as well. I have put self down, or mortified my flesh (Rom. 8:13), and allow Jesus' resurrected life, the Holy Spirit, to be Lord over me as I wait.

Waiting on God can be elusive, discouraging, and overwhelming. We are bound to our flesh, we are afraid of him, and we are afraid of ourselves. Some parts of me are still afraid to let him come, but many parts of me literally have been loved into his presence.

Our part is actually the simplest and yet it has its challenges.

1. We must be still and quiet before the Father, Son, and Holy Spirit. We must do so whether we are studying and poring over the Scriptures or focusing all our attention

on him by simply waiting (Hosea 12:6). Both are powerful, and waiting on God is not either-or, but both-and.
Both are imperative, and they feed one another. If you
cannot do one, do the other.

2. *We must allow him time to rise up, to well up within
our human spirit, to show himself.* Start with five to ten
minutes and gradually work to fifteen or twenty minutes.
Whenever possible, take several hours just to be with
him; those who can give more time should. Being faithful to ten or fifteen minutes a day of waiting on God will
yield great harvests. God has his pattern for you. He
enlarges our time with him as he desires and we are able.
He is never unreasonable (Lam. 3:25–26). There is always
a way, no matter what your schedule may be.

This subject of time is of the essence to waiting. Waiting is time; that is why it is mentioned in each chapter.
Time investment is a necessity. When he becomes important enough to us, we make the needed choices to spend
time with him. Our use of time reveals what is really
important to us!

3. *We must not give up after a few minutes because it is
hard to focus on an invisible Friend within you.* Persist,
persist, and persist. Do not be afraid of fear or of the darkness you may see in yourself. Keep crying out to him.
The name of Jesus on our lips is powerful to cause us to
continue. I do not and cannot make it happen, so I ask
the Holy Spirit to keep me in an effortless mode of receiving from him. And I keep believing and trusting him to do
what is best for me, what I cannot do for myself.

We are more afraid of him than we realize when the
first welling up of his love within us begins. It is sweet to
us, but frightening too, and at first we often cut it off by
getting up, by breaking the focus. We cannot take too
much at first, but we improve as we gain more experience with him. We become less afraid of what he will do
or say (Heb. 4:14–16).

4. We must stay humble before him. Do not talk; listen, be respectful of him, and completely dependent on him. You are helpless. Sink low in submissiveness. Follow his lead the best you can. It is hardest when you first enter into waiting, but over the months and years it becomes easier. Our lives are not our own; they belong to him, Paul tells us in 1 Corinthians 6:19. We have come into his presence by stopping all other activity to focus on him, looking to him, not ourselves, to be in control. Do not be afraid to be brought into such nothingness that you become afraid that you will cease to exist (1 Peter 5:5–6; Isa. 57:15).

5. We must believe that he will come, and we must not fret over distractions. Simply bring your mind back again to him. If a particular distraction keeps recurring, ask the Holy Spirit to reveal what he is seeking to say to you through it. Many times guilt and conflict will emerge over and over until we deal with some particular issue. Andrew Murray stresses in his book *Waiting on God* the theme that we are to trust God that he will come to us. This fact has helped me so much. I often declare out loud, "Lord, you have come, you shall come, you will come. Thank you, Father; thank you, Jesus; thank you, Holy Spirit" (John 14:18).

As we wait he empowers us to walk in obedience to what he has revealed.

He Pierces, Divides, and Discerns

It is a recurrent tragedy of our race that we do not realize the sinfulness of sin. . . . We call our sins "mistakes," "weaknesses," "slips"—Sin is deadly.

William Sangster

There are two major ways to wait on God to receive the promise of the Father, the unspeakable gift of the Holy Spirit to change our lives.

The first is sitting quietly, closing our eyes to external distractions, and focusing our inner attention upon Jesus. We begin then to listen humbly to what he may say to us.

The second way is the theme of this chapter. When I first started waiting on God years ago, I found that one of the most satisfactory ways to focus on Jesus within me is to ask the Holy Spirit to open the Scriptures to me as I sit quietly and ponder them. I knew the Holy Spirit had inspired men to write the Word of God, and I took seriously 2 Timothy 3:16–17: "All Scripture is given by inspiration of God, and is profitable for doctrine, for reproof, for correction, for instruction in righteousness: that the man of God may be perfect, thoroughly furnished unto all good works."

God was teaching me to defer to him in our time together. I would ask the Holy Spirit to make alive and real the Scripture reading and would slowly, carefully ponder what I was reading, aided by the indwelling Holy Spirit. He was training my spiritual ears to grasp the understanding of what I was reading. Verses 4 and 5 of Isaiah 50 suddenly came to my awareness, "He wakeneth morning by morning, he wakeneth mine ear to hear as the learned. The Lord GOD hath opened mine ear, and I was not rebellious, neither turned away back."

My life was filled with diverse experiences, yet they were unified because the Holy Spirit was teaching me how to keep the spiritual dimension central to all my involvements. I was teaching in a college, attending university classes for a degree in marital and family therapy, and involved in my church. I had consecrated my life to him a few years before; I had received the Holy Spirit in a life-changing way; I was spending time daily with God and loved poring over the Scriptures. The praying community to which I belonged was seeing answers to prayer. I was walking with God the best I knew how.

But God had an illuminating experience waiting for me one morning (Jer. 17:9–10). One of the delights of walking with him is the unexpected joy of his spontaneity at every turn. I was meditating on Isaiah 66:2. "To this man will I look, even to him that is poor and of contrite spirit, and trembleth at my word." Over the years the Holy Spirit had revealed to me through conversations with my parents and friends that my soulish realm (flesh) was very strong willed. Thus far, however, the dark and treacherous side of my self-will had not been under the light of the Holy Spirit. On this particular day I had an unusually profound awareness, as God's Word rose up before me, that my tendency to act out of my emotional life rather than the Holy Spirit was so common I did not know the difference. A part of me did not tremble enough at his Word. I was defensive and self-protective. It began to dawn on me how opposite my soul realm was to Isaiah 66:2. I was shocked at how much I did out of the strong energies of the soul, as opposed to being so in awe at his Word that I waited to act until it was clear to me. How prone to going out on my own I was (Gal. 5:16–26). The Holy Spirit showed me how the soul realm loves not only to be strong in its energies but religious in its activities. Energies of the soul take over the power and place of the Holy Spirit, masquerading as his substitute.

So much of what I was doing came from my best judgment, not that of the Word of the Lord. It was what Margaret said, and not what God said. He revealed to me as I waited on him in his Word how easily I fell into the emotions of superiority and pride in my self-righteousness. What pomp and fury of self I displayed (Rom. 7:14–24)! I saw clearly the spiritual pride that is such an abomination to God (Job 19:28).

Further, I remembered that during the previous Sunday worship service at our church, the Holy Spirit had said, "Don't judge anyone else around you. You have lived as soulishly and selfishly as anyone in this church. You are caught in emotional bondage and prideful ways of thinking. You need to tremble at my Word!"

I was too full of myself, but suddenly I saw it! The depth of my soulishness and self-bias frightened me. It was as if the dear Spirit of Jesus took off the lid and let me take a long look down into all the awful filth and mire (Matt. 15:18–19; Rom. 3:10–19). I saw the battlefield of the enormous powers of the flesh with its energies of self-flattery and self-deception. He caused me to see the terribleness of sin (John 16:7–12).

It all looked hopeless to me. He separated the motivation of my soul from my spirit. I saw the difference between the two. I was so conditioned to producing out of my own energy what I felt needed to be done, and when it should be done. How parts of me resisted denying myself, taking the lowly place, picking up the cross of selflessness. I felt trapped, unable to make any change, struggling between the self-advantage of the flesh and the pure ways of Spirit, as described in the seventh chapter of Romans. Never had I seen the division more clearly; I was grateful for the convicting power of the Holy Spirit.

From this dark despair my heart cried out, "Help me, Lord Jesus, I cannot help myself. Come and help me, Jesus. Only you can make a real change here, only you." Heretofore I had always assumed I could fix my spiritual dilemmas, change them, make them right. In a flash I saw that the same light showing me my darkness was the light that would allow him to redeem any situation.

But out of that penetrating self-knowledge, I saw how helpless and powerless I was. There was no possible way to improve or change myself. This opening up of my soul had brought me so low I found myself in a new place of humility. I *did* tremble at his Word. I saw my inner poverty in a whole new way, in the flesh, and saw that in the soul realm there was nothing I could do for or in myself! I knew the deepest issue for me would be ceasing to operate out of the realm of the soul, where I am in the driver's seat, and allowing God the Holy Spirit to rule and reign within my soul and spirit.

In those minutes God, through the Holy Spirit's illumination, let me get a good, hard look at what my flesh was all about. He let the message sink in deeply: Nothing I could do would alter my self-focus.

Deep in my human spirit, the Holy Spirit began to speak. "The depth of your soulishness is frightening, but you must see this raw material of self because it drives you to me. There is nothing you can do except acknowledge the truth and repent. The deepest prayer you can pray is, 'Lord, I die to self, to ego, to my willpower, to my self-sufficiency, to this awful sin of putting myself first. Crucify all that is unlike you.'" And having seen my awful predicament, I wanted the Holy Spirit to be in control. I realized I would be requesting his control for the rest of my life as he exposed other deep needs. Only through daily lingering in his presence can he continually bring to death in me the sin of rebellion against his authority. What a shock to see how we contaminate our life with God with such self-protectiveness.

The pain of all this was unlike any other time in his presence, but I knew God the Holy Spirit was at work in me. We need these painful but rich revelations to see our true condition. It is truly a work of the Holy Spirit to reveal our inner attitudes as we begin to wait on God.

Next, he brought to my mind Paul's saying, "I die daily" (1 Cor. 15:31). In other words, Paul said no to self-rule. It began to burn within me that waiting on God, denying the ways of human personality and human strength, was a way to turn daily from self-focus to God the Father, Son, and Holy Spirit. And I had been praying for some time for God, at any cost, to get hold of my flesh as never before!

I saw in the waiting that I began deliberately turning from self-preservation and self-orientation and looking at Jesus, rather than looking at myself. Pondering the Word of God was a way of forgetting about myself and becoming absorbed in what he had to tell me. Waiting, then, could be called a form of self-denial, a dying to self, a daily humbling of my selfhood in his presence. For a specific time period each day, at least, I lay down all rights to myself and wait for him to speak and to be Lord of my life. Jesus says at four different places in Scripture that we are to deny ourselves, take up the cross, and follow him. Taking the cross means I say no to my self-will and yes to his will. The carnal, fleshly part of us does not want to be denied, does not want to say no to self-will; it wants to follow Jesus the way *we* want to follow Jesus. It is my deepest conviction that the "how" of Matthew 10:37–39, Matthew 16:24–25, Mark 8:34–35, and Luke 9:23–25 is in waiting daily. I allow God access to my time (self-will) and to my desires (self-love), two of the defining parts of the soul realm. The soulish realm says, "I will do what I want to do when I want to do it." Waiting means refusing to allow self to have its way in this period of time.

Jesus spent much time alone with the Father and the Holy Spirit. He chose to be helpless, powerless, dependent on the Father through the Holy Spirit, and he was God himself! How he modeled surrender to the Father! He says over and over in the following passages, "I am dependent on God the Father through the Holy Spirit."

John 5:19, 30
John 6:38, 57
John 7:28
John 8:28, 42
John 12:44–45

Scripture gives us ten accounts in the Gospel of Luke alone where Jesus went off to be with God the Father. If getting away to wait on and for God was necessary for him, how much more necessary it is for you and me!

The pattern of saying no to self becomes stronger in us through repeated waiting. And this same humbling begins to seep out into the other hours of the day. The goal of waiting is to allow him to be in control all through the day and not just in my waiting time. I do not believe, nor have I ever seen it lived out, that all dying to self is accomplished in one fell swoop, through one singular spiritual experience. We may have one experience where we say yes to his purifying fires, but we must surrender totally and yield daily, even moment by moment, if we desire to live within his holy nature.

Some years before the experience of which I just wrote, the Holy Spirit, when he came to me to baptize me in God's love, did a life-changing thing in me by burning dross from my emotions, mind, and will. I literally felt as if I were burning up for four days, the first being the most intense. As a result of that experience, I had no anger, no resentment, no unforgiveness, no envy, no jealousy for one year. But then these sins began recurring, even though I was spending time each day with God. I was shattered and called my mother. She said, "You have experienced the burning fire of the Holy Spirit (Luke 3:16–17), and he has removed much dross from you. But now you are to cooperate more intentionally by waiting on him, giving him the freedom to expose whatever sins of the flesh and spirit he sees (2 Cor. 7:1). When he does, repent quickly (Rev. 3:19), be cleansed, and go on. This is giving him lordship in you, to purify and bring you more into obedience and victory." Mother also told me that God was teaching me to be willingly helpless and dependent on God's life in me.

That fiery experience with the Holy Spirit, its aftermath, and my mother's counsel really propelled me into waiting on God. We all have areas in our souls and spirits as yet untouched by him, but as we gaze lovingly on him, giving him our undivided attention, he begins lovingly and correctively to bring these levels to our view. We cannot give him what we do not see (Ps. 51:6)! He yearns to draw out of our hidden parts the truth, to integrate our souls and spirits under his dominion so we have no inner conflicts.

This mysterious, yet oh so real inner working of the Holy Spirit is a great mystery, and it plumbs many levels of our inner being. Not only do we begin to see our neediness, our poverty of soul and spirit, but as he is more active in every part of us, our waiting allows him to begin stripping away our artificial self, through not allowing the sinful, soulish self to be in control. As he emerges he throws light on our emotional woundedness and the harshness of our personalities. We give him access into who we are. At the outset we do not know who we are. This kind of waiting is so painful and is sometimes nearly impossible. I have cried out to God many times, "I don't want to deal with this . . . I won't . . . I won't . . ." Yet, by the power of the blood of Jesus Christ, I will not allow myself to run away.

The dividing of our soul and spirit, so we can even begin to understand where we actually are, can only be done through and in the Holy Spirit. He begins to do amazing things within. He comes as fire to burn and convict and empower us to repent with gut-level seriousness!

We do not want sin to separate us from him even for an instant. We yearn to be in his love nature and abide there, not to be trapped in our selfishness. We are embarking on a lifetime journey of transformation into the authentic, non-imitative persons he wants us to be.

When we say no to self in prayer and waiting, we experience a death to this soulish, lesser self. This death allows the indwelling Spirit to come alive in us. He has been there all the time, but our soulish realm pushes him out of the driver's seat. The Holy Spirit, the resurrected life of God, takes supremacy and begins to empower us to say no to ourselves during the day. This means, for example, that if the Holy Spirit has shown you that you are talking too much during the day, drawing attention to yourself, you say to the Holy Spirit, "Help me to keep my lips closed and take a less conspicuous place." And he does.

I believe the lost message of transformation to his image is revealed in all the Scripture mentioned thus far. As we wait, the inner work of the Holy Spirit is released. He corrects us, brings us to Jesus to be cleansed by his blood, and leads us into repentance or death to our sins. Repentance always brings the life of the Holy Spirit in all his resurrection power and love (Acts 2:38).

Psalm 139:23–24 says, "Search me, O God, and know my heart; try me and know my thoughts: and see if there be any wicked way in me, and lead me in the way everlasting." I do truly understand the unspeakable import of what is expressed in these verses. The very essence of sin in my ego, the *I,* the *me,* the *my,* must continually be cleansed by the Holy Spirit. This cleansing is done daily as he pierces, divides, and discerns my secret thoughts and nature (Hebrews 4). As Jessie Penn-Lewis writes, "The 'works of the flesh,' it penetrates into the realm of the affections, and shows itself in self-love, self-pity, self-grasping, and other phases of self-centeredness. This must be called *sin,* although in less discernible form, working through intellect, emotions and affections."[9]

To the depth that we daily humble ourselves before God Almighty, to that depth our self-centeredness will be under his control throughout the day. It is hard to bring it under control amidst the intensities of daily experience if it has not been brought under in a specific time with God. In laying down how we would live our own lives out of our own will, and wanting him to live his life more strongly in us, we say no to our selfishness. In John 12:24–26 Jesus says that unless we are willing to die, we remain alone and unfruitful, carnal, fleshly. We have a fierce loneliness within because we are trying to meet the need outside of the presence of Jesus. The need is met only through saying no to self. This allows the part of us carved out by God for himself to be filled by simply "being" in his presence.

Human experiences teach us, and trial and difficulty humble us, but I truly believe the way he wants to humble us is in our daily time of being shut in with him, pondering his Word or simply waiting for him to speak in our spirits. We must give him permission to separate our dark carnal selves, our soul, from our spirit so we can move into more honesty about ourselves.

A dear friend confessed that the circumstances of her life were so furious and fast that she had little time to wait. "I've noticed a distinct difference in my anger level," she said, "and I have not been nearly as patient as when I am allowing God to deal with me, quietly giving him my undivided attention in waiting."

We will find that as we wait on God, through meditating on Scripture and in quiet listening, many powerful things begin to happen within. We will begin to love him so deeply that we will yearn for deep personal holiness. We will long to be emptied out of all that offends him so we can be filled afresh and anew with him. There is one baptism, but we can enjoy many fillings of his precious Spirit each and every day. Charles Spurgeon wrote, "I cannot overcome myself, nor overcome my sin. I will never cease from the task, God helping me, but apart from the Divine Spirit the task is as impossible as to make a world."[10]

God will never be content, nor should we be content, until he has control over the entire soulish realm and in our human spirit.

The inner journey with God is an unbelievable saga. I love the stories of the westward migration in the United States, but the inner migration to union with Jesus is the greatest of all journeys! Only the Godhead knows all the penetrating work necessary to change us into his image. He constantly molds us to the degree we allow him to work.

But our time with God can prove to be a royal battle because the self-orientation in us does not want to yield its authority to God. We will have many failures, but they will help us experience the depth of our selfhood and its strength. Repentance will become a recurring theme of our time with him. But if we persist he will teach us and we will yearn beyond expression to please him above all else.

Philippians 2:1–15 reveals the unspeakable submission and humbling of Jesus as he left heaven and yielded to the lowliness of obedience, even to death on the cross. The inner ministry of the Holy Spirit instills Jesus' lowliness and submissive obedience in us as we humbly wait on him.

God's Commitment

1. *Jesus understands our sin and our weaknesses and will give us mercy and grace as we come to him.* The role of Jesus Christ as our high and exalted priest is highlighted in the fourth chapter of the Book of Hebrews. I believe this entire chapter is a pattern for our daily coming into the Holy of Holies, our heart, where he as High Priest resides. For not only is he priest over the sanctuary in the heavens, but he is our priest, as the indwelling Christ, in the sanctuary of our hearts (Heb. 8:1–2).

2. *The Holy Spirit will make the written Word pierce and divide our soul realm from the spirit realm (Heb. 4:12).* Asking him to quicken the Word as we ponder its meaning is one of the most powerful ways to wait on God. That is what was happening to me as I read Isaiah 66:2. The Holy Spirit began to penetrate, pierce, and divide my emotions and reveal them to me so I could see them as they were. We need him to do this daily because we are such complex people; our tendency is to deny and bury so much of what we feel. The Holy Spirit, the Helper, helps us to see clearly our true condition.

Hebrews 4 speaks not only of the rest of being redeemed and in God's family but also of the rest of being at peace with him and having him reside within us. I was not at rest emotionally, though my salvation was intact. I was unaware of what my emotions were saying to me; I had no idea that my self-will was so strong. We need time with Jesus because we do not know the depth of our emotional frailty.

3. If we give him permission, the Holy Spirit will, if necessary, wrench the soul from the spirit so we can see the difference between these two distinct areas of our makeup. We have no idea how much the soulish realm rules over us. We are overdeveloped in self-reliance and self-realization, leaning completely on our talents, resources, education, and works. Prayerful waiting allows the Holy Spirit to plunge the knife and separate the soulish from the spiritual so we can see each for what it truly is. He lifts up our emotions so we can see them and call them by name. He does not want us to sugarcoat emotions such as anger, resentment, and unforgiveness. We need to see sin as sin.

Romans 7:22 says, "For I delight in the law of God after the inward man." God allows the Word of God to pierce and separate our emotions so we can see things as they really are. As we ponder and wait, open to his leading as our teacher, he will cut to the heart of all situations and all personal issues if we will let him. He reveals our true attitudes in both the soul and spirit realm.

4. God ever wants to broaden our knowledge and understanding of ourselves and of him. The older we become the more transparent our needs become in the face of him. He is never more of a comforter than when he lovingly deals with our sin.

But this is possible only as we give him permission to discern our true situations. Often the thoughts and intents of our souls and spirits are so buried and hidden we cannot know them. "The Comforter . . . shall teach you all things" (John 14:26). To allow the Holy Spirit to search us so we can be emptied of unconfessed sin is to be cleansed and healed.

5. We do not have to fear what he will show us, for he will reveal only what we can bear. As we gain in experience with our wonderful Teacher, he will, as we allow him, reveal more and more of our soulish realm and more and more of himself as the answer to our need. Ours will be an ever-expanding communion.

6. He will never condemn us, but will always pour on the love as he corrects. Many times he reveals that our intentions and motivations of spirit are honest and open, more desirous of him than our self-driven, demanding, soulish, ego-centered realms. Our emotional lives, so wounded and bruised, often may feel condemnation and think that it comes from the Holy Spirit. He never condemns us! His love always affirms and never condemns (Rom. 8:1). We condemn ourselves based on emotional responses of rejection and misunderstanding learned in childhood and projected from the soulish realm. Satan loves to fan the fires of what we think is God's rejection.

One time when the Holy Spirit was dividing my soul and spirit, he taught me what was happening in my emotions and mind and showed me how to overcome the pitfall of condemnation. I believe only the Holy Spirit can reveal to each believer, unique as we are, how to overcome condemnation's devastation. But as we wait and ponder his Word, he will show us!

7. Our emotional life is potent, but he will also throw his light on our thinking processes, including the area of imagination. Our imaginations must be reclaimed by the Holy Spirit, cleansed, and taught to fix on Jesus and his mind. He reveals distortions in our thinking, such as lack of trust in what God can do. He can reveal how oversensitive we are about our opinions. He can reveal how negative our thinking is at times. He will make us aware of how bound to fear we are in much of our thinking. We can try to know God strictly through the intellect or reasoning, but the Scriptures say that our thinking is to be transformed by the renewing of the mind (Rom. 12:2). As we reflect or meditate on the Word of God our way of thinking is altered.

A beautiful young woman told me recently that as she waited on God through the Scripture the Holy Spirit revealed to her a self-destructive and faulty thinking pattern she had never seen before, a pattern of doubt and unbelief that Jesus would help her to overcome if she would allow him. Many people had tried to show her this error, but she could not see it. As she waited daily, which was a new spiritual experience for her, the Holy Spirit separated and lifted up her emotions. For the first time she could see them for what they were, and she truly repented. She has asked the Holy Spirit to help her change her sinful habit, to convict her on the spot each time she falls into it. She was willing to make audible restitution as the Holy Spirit guided her.

8. One of the Holy Spirit's main tasks is to get us out of soulish, emotional thinking to a purer level, a level where we think more like he does. The depth of our pride and defensiveness goes deep. He has shown me how I want to "save face" at nearly any cost! He reveals our self-serving ways so we can see them and repent. He shows us how we are enslaved to our feelings and sinful thought processes, believing lies rather than his truth, and not even knowing the difference! He must pierce deeply to break our allegiance to the soulish realm and so we can see the truth as he reveals it.

I know a woman in our praying community who is faithful to waiting on God in the several hours she spends each day with him.

"Margaret," she told me, "I've had to speak some things to my family and I know I am right!"

"All right," I said. She seemed agitated, emotionally heated, but I know her heart is responsive to God.

Several days later she said, "Well, I was right in what I said but wrong in my attitude as I said it, so I've had to go back and make amends."

"How did you come to that awareness?" I asked.

"As I spent time in the Scriptures, waiting on God, he revealed that I had spoken in anger and accusation, so I was wrong. I have had to go back to each family member and ask forgiveness for my terrible anger."

9. *God is faithful to pierce, divide, and interpret so we can learn the difference between living the Christian life out of sensual self-love and the love of the Holy Spirit.* Hebrews 12 speaks about our need for corrective chastening, subduing, or restraining so that we might partake of his holiness, his purity (v. 10). We are not sons and daughters of the Most High God if we refuse to allow him to correct us (v. 8). Sometimes his correction must be forceful, because we are so strong willed. He scourges us or deals with us severely!

I believe with all my heart that the devotional life of prayer and waiting on God allows him to deal with us as his children, cleansing away any bitterness of sin on a daily basis. This daily revealing as we wait and ponder his Word causes us to get rid of sin in our emotional attitudes or mental outlooks. Bitterness, which is so dangerous to us all, is not allowed to rule over us because we are in God's presence long enough to receive his loving correction and move into the freedom his sons and daughters should enjoy.

But without daily openness to his Word and his Spirit, we live our lives mainly in the soulish realm and wonder why we have so little victory. Job 34:31–32 says, "Surely it is meet to be said unto God, I have borne chastisement, I will not offend any more: That *which I see not teach thou me:* if I have done iniquity, I will do no more" (emphasis added). Verse 27 speaks of individuals who took a different attitude: "they turned back from him, and would not consider any of his ways." Unlike Job, these persons refused to see, to let God reveal the truth.

Daily, leisurely time alone with God allows the Holy Spirit to reveal, confront, correct, and empower us to "turn from [our] wicked ways" (Ezek. 3:19) with godly repentance (2 Cor. 7:10). Without appropriating his grace and mercy and moving into pronounced honesty, we are left crippled and in bondage.

10. The Holy Spirit longs to show us the rest that is available to us when our high priest, Jesus, is allowed to be high priest in our lives. Many Christians have never been taught the role of the indwelling Holy Spirit. Many have never waited on God so he could help them. Many have never realized their tremendous neediness and have lived their whole Christian lives burdened with the same crippling personal issues. Many are out of touch with their emotional or mental sins and dysfunction; if given daily time with God, they would and could be healed.

No wonder Satan has so maligned the inner ministry of the Holy Spirit. He has been ignored, neglected, made fun of, and minimized. Yet the truth is that the only person that can live the Christian life is the person of the Holy Spirit within me. As we spiritually process the insights gleaned through his piercing and discerning, we develop a growing intimacy with the Father, Son, and Holy Spirit. Working in and through each episode brings great peace and rest, plus a more powerful sense that he loves us and helps us in that love. We know him better and know ourselves better, and he builds in us compassion for others and ourselves.

Many consecrated Christians today have little, if any, confidence in the working of the Holy Spirit within them. Their Christian lives are predominately external, self-sustaining out of the soulish realm, and lived in defeat and unawareness because they are trying to live the life themselves. The Holy Spirit wants to release the power of Jesus to live his life through them and through us.

I believe holiness unto the Lord is loving him so totally, in a growing way, that I come to my place of waiting on him daily with an ever-increasing desire for him. As I grant permission for him to take control, to reveal whatever I need to see, and to lead me to heartfelt repentance. I say no to acting out of emotions, personality, and will. He also reveals my faulty thinking. His correction brings life.

Our Commitment

For centuries the great saints have written that coming into God's presence and waiting quietly is the highest level of activity humans can know. I believe this is so because waiting opens the door to divine action. Scripture bears this out, over and over; Isaiah 30:7, for example, says, "their strength is to sit still."

We fail to realize all he must do within to make us into the image of Jesus. As we begin to wait on him, we begin to see him more clearly, and we see the depth of change that must be made in us. The sinful stains of self-effort (energy) and self-bias (attitude) go to the core of who we are in our humanity. The soul life does not want to let go of being the all in all. In his book *The Spiritual Man* Watchman Nee says, "The soul life seeks to serve God, but it will always be according to the soul's ideas, not according to God's ideas. It will always seek to oppose and quench the Holy Spirit by leaning upon its own strength without wholly relying upon God's grace. The soulish realm has enormous energies of self-will. Self-pity, self-love, fear of suffering, with a prime motivation being self-preservation are all qualities of the soul that must be cleansed. It will always fight against taking the cross and dying to self-centeredness. Only the Holy Spirit, through prayer, can empower us to die to self-will."[11]

In other words our needs are huge, far greater than we can know in self-knowledge outside the Holy Spirit. Saint Teresa of Avila once said, "How I fail, how I fail, how I fail, and I could say it a thousand times—to get rid of everything for you."[12]

Our greatest need, therefore, is an increased willingness to be open and humble as we spend time in waiting. This is not easy, especially once we begin to experience his piercing and interpreting of our inner man. We will want to stop because the pain is great. But oh, the joy of understanding as we allow him to help us. He is so tender, so kind, so healing to all our being as we allow him to highlight the "pet idolatries" and emotional substitutes that are hindering our intimacy with him. It is a joy to respond to his loving but serious correction of what has been so destructive and harmful in our lives. Beware of thinking that you know better than the Holy Spirit and pulling back from following him. He will reveal basic issues in our lives as we wait, and he will give us strength to go on.

1. One aspect of our commitment is to have courage for this great, inner journey with the Holy Spirit. The Holy Spirit will give us the courage we need as we need it, if we are daily coming to him—waiting, listening, and poring over the Scriptures. His life in us will be brought forth as we gaze upon him in and through the Bible. This is the unbelievable power of the resurrection, the Holy Spirit, made available to us as we appropriate him in waiting (Ps. 33:20–21).

It takes courage to wait on God, to set aside time to face our creatureliness and inner poverty, to cease for a time to operate out of all forms of self, and to embrace our inner darkness rather than denying it. But we will have to face these realities sometime; it might as well be sooner as later, especially since he longs to help and is so available to us.

2. We also need to accept, not resist, his help as he reveals more of ourselves to us. If we run from seeing the self-dependency that seeks to substitute for the power of the Holy Spirit, our lives will never become "the new creation" referred to in Galatians 6:15. The "new creation" is a person daily emptied out of self-absorption and its workings so that the life of God within can gain supremacy over the soulish realm. Then we can begin to live out of the Holy Spirit active in our human spirit, rather than out of self and the power of egocentrism. Continuing to focus on ourselves is death.

As we wait, he steps forward and lives his life more powerfully in us. As Galatians 2:20 says, "I am crucified with Christ, nevertheless I live." When our human egos are no longer in control but laid aside, Christ *can* live in and through us, and "[we] do not frustrate the grace of God" (v. 21). We respond, that is, to his way of doing things.

Second Corinthians 4:10 says that we need to be "always bearing about in the body the dying of the Lord Jesus, that the life also of Jesus might be made manifest in our body." This means that we identify with his death in the losing of our lives, letting them go, that his life may have freedom within us.

3. We need to be willing to come against the self by not operating in that mode during our time with God. Denial of self, practiced in time alone with God so we can learn to maintain it all through the day, is a whole new way of life. It is exciting, releasing, and fulfilling to wait for him to take over, to speak, to lead, rather than to act out of my best educated guess! The thrill of his life intermingling with mine and of allowing him to be Lord is humbling indeed.

Luke 5 gives a perfect example of how much more effective it is to hear from Jesus first before dashing out to act on our own. "Launch out into the deep, and let down your nets," Jesus told Simon Peter one day. "Master," said Peter, "we have toiled all the night, and have taken nothing: nevertheless at thy word I will let down the net." The net was not only filled, but to the breaking point! Peter's self-effort produced nothing, but his obedience to Jesus' word produced abundance.

The challenge on our part is to be increasingly open and responsive in allowing the Holy Spirit to reveal our utter helplessness. We cannot control him by our waiting; we can only receive from him whatever he wants to give (Ps. 145:15–21). In the waiting time, we are practicing laying down our interests and our will in deference to his interests and his will. This is a new role for us. Remember, Jesus chose helplessness and powerlessness that the Father might work through him. He is our role model for being willing to accomplish nothing unless a work is of God's doing (John 5:19, 30; 8:28–29).

4. We also must commit to growing humility in our time with God, and more meekness and lowliness in all our attitudes. Andrew Murray says, "Learn to say of every want and every failure and every lack of needful grace: I have waited too little upon God or He would have given me in due season all I needed."[13]

The older I become the more total my dependency on him is and should be; and the more he should be seen in me. Here again, I want to say how poorly I have appropriated the grace of God in all my waiting. The wonder is that the Holy Spirit has poured himself out so generously in comparison to how pathetic I have been in getting out of his way. He seems to love any attempt I make to be quiet and still before him, and he honors his Word in merciful ways more generously than we can understand. The joy of seeing his presence become more real is the sweetest outcome of waiting, and he gives it lavishly no matter how poor our attempts at waiting.

The challenge is to ever-deeper submission of all self-life to the Son of God, practiced faithfully day after day. To pull apart from the external living which so dominates our lives, stopping all action, and humbly stilling ourselves to behold him is to draw closer to the indwelling Holy Spirit. He helps us to be more and more willing to draw apart with him by bringing disappointment and dissatisfaction with our "achievements" in the external world. We feel those achievements should bring more fulfillment than they do. But increasingly we find that what comes out of our own strength and our own direction never truly satisfies; because only he can satisfy (Ps. 107:9).

To be daily in the Scriptures, waiting on the Holy Spirit to pierce, divide, and discern our intents and motivations, is not a quick and easy process. But giving the time necessary, in a submissive attitude, to poring over the Scriptures becomes part and parcel of my willingness to be clay in the Potter's hands. I cannot state this too strongly. Almost the last words my mother spoke to me were, "You must spend more time in the Word of God." I have taken her admonition seriously.

5. *If we find that we need human help, we need to pray that God will make a mature Christian person available.* There is much emphasis today on counseling and therapy to help individuals with their problems. And indeed, the Scriptures speak of those who are older and wiser helping those who are younger. Titus 2 urges older men and women to teach younger men and women about living godly lives (vv. 1–8). I believe profoundly in this biblical principle, but its practice is sadly missing in many lives today. The nurturing, affirming, correcting, and loving from such exchanges is powerful and desperately needed.

I believe counseling and therapy are valid ways to help people deal with their selfishness and woundedness if done in a Christian context. The Bible says that in the multitude of counselors there is safety (Prov. 11:14). It is good to go to others, particularly the younger to the older, but I am afraid we have not taught people the biblical injunction to come to Jesus directly and learn from him (John 5:40–44). Unfortunately, we usually will go to anyone else rather than come to the dear Holy Spirit. Our churches are filled with people who attend every service but feel inadequate to get to God, much less hear him speak to them. Many feel, in fact, that they cannot experience intimacy with him at all.

These dear believers have never heard about waiting on God. In John 10:3 Jesus speaks of how sheep hear the shepherd's voice, "and he calleth his own sheep by name, and leadeth them out." Verses 4 and 5 go on: "The sheep follow him: for they know his voice. And a stranger will they not follow, but will flee from him: for they know not the voice of strangers." Jesus adds, "I am the good shepherd, and know my sheep, and am known of mine" (v. 14).

As a marriage and family therapist, I see many people who confuse the voices within them and call any voice God. I fully realize the danger of unstable people "hearing" from God. Nothing has done more damage to this biblical concept of waiting than news reports about unbalanced people who think they have "a word from God" and go off in all directions. But this is why the young and inexperienced in waiting and listening need someone more mature and experienced to help them test out their findings as to whether God has spoken. Balance, insight, teaching, a passing of the faith to another, and correction usually result.

Many people, unable to go to God and wait because they lack teaching and spiritual guidance, live unfulfilled, impersonal, remote lives with God. The dangers of never waiting are far more severe than those that result from trying to wait, even "poorly." It is amazing how marvelously God will guide, direct, and accompany Christians through circumstances, a little devotional life, and a shadow of listening and waiting. But he has spread a banquet table for us. How pitiful it is to live on bread and water when milk and honey could be ours! He longs for us to come (Song of Sol. 2:4).

The more we are emptied of ourselves as we wait before God, the more he deepens our capacity to receive from God. In closing this chapter I suggest you begin with five to ten minutes of waiting each day. After a few weeks or months add five more minutes, and then another five to ten. Twenty to thirty minutes of waiting on God during your quiet time each day will be life changing, bringing returns in all areas of your life.

Living Out
the Waiting

In your patience possess ye your soul.

Luke 21:19

I could identify heartily with the earnest young man in my office as he explained the grief he felt in allowing "office frenzy" to pull him into confusion and anxiety. He knew that such confusion was a far cry from the serenity and peace that characterize the indwelling Holy Spirit.

"My prayer and waiting time are so healing to me. Jesus is real, but when I step into my office and go to work, I am trapped again and again in failure and despair. I know I leave Jesus at my prayer and waiting time, and go back into my strong personality and self-will. There has to be an answer to this! How can these two realms be united?"

I understood what he was saying. In the early days of my waiting on God I felt so good about our hour or hour and a half early in the morning. Many times, however, I was in defeat by noon and no longer at peace within. I had talked too much, offering my "priceless" opinions and strong feelings when I should have listened and spoken with more compassion and kindness. Living out of our personalities is second nature to us because we have done it all our lives. It takes more of Jesus than we realize for him to have the control and dominion over our self-assertiveness. But as we begin to give him time in waiting daily, the fountain of his grace and mercy begins to flow (Jer. 2:13; Isa. 27:3).

I often found an ugly part of me surfacing as I attended meetings, for example. My ego and soulish realm would take over. Thoughts would enter my mind and words would come out of my mouth that astonished me. Had I not spent time with God that morning? Yet my words reflected not the love of God but my own self-focus.

Nothing shocks, discourages, and grieves the earnest Christian more than the sin of self. But I was so used to taking over through my personality and will, and the habit continued even after a life-changing experience with the Holy Spirit and a surrender of my life and will. After my life-changing experience there was a season when he was more in control, but I continued to have times of great failure over which I wept.

One morning during my quiet time he guided me to meditate on Psalm 46:10: "Be still, and know that I am God." The blessed Holy Spirit revealed to me that only when I remained in his presence of quiet peace continually throughout the day could he reveal his nature so I could experience him in those parts of me that remained untouched and unfulfilled in him. He shined his light on my understanding, teaching me that waiting in quietness and calm was intended not only for my devotional time each morning but also as my chief posture all through the day! What a shock it was to give up the freedom of speech and action that I felt were my due! I did not think I could submit to that depth.

"I want you to refrain from expressing how you feel about everything for a week," said the Holy Spirit. "Continue your quiet reverence in being still before me not just in this time, but stay humble and quiet all day. I will give you permission to speak, but only when I can trust you to let it be me and not you."

"Yes, but, Lord, some people value my opinions," I responded. "They will think I am not interested if I do not give my view on everything. They expect me to speak up!"

"What they think is of no consequence. I want obedience from you," he persisted. "Let the silence and quiet of your intentional waiting extend throughout the day for a week. Keep your mouth closed and listen to me in your heart. Let others talk more and you less!"

That assignment just about killed me! Colleagues thought I was sick, losing my grip. They turned to me, waiting for my forceful edicts. At first I would automatically launch out, but the Holy Spirit would prick me to remember our covenant of quiet waiting for a week, and I would quickly close my mouth, apologizing for speaking so forcefully. I learned to respond, "I am more interested in hearing from you."

By the fourth or fifth day I felt relief at not having to set everyone straight. The most thrilling thing I experienced was that God was giving me such peace. His presence continued to be strong and sweet in me, not just in my devotional time but during every moment of the day.

"Are you fighting the flu, or what?" one friend asked late in the week.

"No, physically I am fine, but the Holy Spirit has told me to be quiet and responsive to him, and I can only do that by talking much less!"

"Oh, I thought something terrible had happened!" My friend had no idea of the impact this assignment had on me and the changes it was making in my life. The week finally ended. It had seemed longer than seven days, and I said to the Holy Spirit, "Lord, that was really hard. I'm sure glad it's over. I know it did me good, though I didn't enjoy it much. I don't know how successful it was, but at least I tried. Now we can go onto something else, right?"

"As a matter of fact, I enjoyed it tremendously; let's go another week," came the Lord's reply. "Let's add something else to this mortification of the tongue; let's not go into the faculty room at noon for the rest of the year. You are acting out of your emotions, rather than being in me, all the time you are there. You are speaking harshly and critically. It is harmful to me, to you, and to your prayer life. I want you to stay away from that room for a long time."

How his words pierced my heart! And how true they were! My need to have the last word was so strong. I had left the faculty room many times stricken and corrected by the Holy Spirit, and I repeatedly had to make restitution to my colleagues. My record showed one inappropriate episode after another.

The Holy Spirit brought Hosea 12:6 to my mind: "Wait on thy God *continually*" (emphasis added). It swept over me that waiting on God was not just a onetime experience in the morning; it involved allowing the Holy Spirit time and place in my attention moment by moment. In this way I would not live out of my emotions and mental processes. Rather, he would be able to guide me moment by moment. He would speak to me and through me continually, pouring out his love in me and through this vessel, my personality. He wanted me to submit to him not just for a short period of time daily but all day, every day.

"You mean I can stay in the Holy of Holies all day long? That is really possible?" I asked.

"Yes," he replied, "it is part of your inheritance (Ps. 47:4). I am always there for you. Let me teach you how to abide in my holy place all day long. When you come to me in the morning you will not be coming such long distances, as you will have ceased from going your own way all the other hours of the day. It takes you so long to be aware of my presence because you have been out in a 'far country' on your own (Luke 15:11–20). You will have much failure, but even that will draw you back to me in humility because you cannot do this in the flesh. It is my work to teach you how to 'abide.'"

The Holy Spirit was speaking of "abiding," or remaining in Jesus' love nature all day, just as a branch never voluntarily cuts itself off from the rooted vine but is permanently fixed. The promise of abiding in him and he in us, as found in John 15, is for every believer, not just for a few.

As all of this was happening, I remembered Frank Laubach's *Game with Minutes* and Brother Lawrence's *Practicing the Presence.* I had always felt these men must be superior, or super-Christians, to be able to live the kind of life they wrote about. But the Holy Spirit spoke deep in my heart, "A new and living way is opened up to all believers, a blood-bought way. You can draw near in full assurance of faith. I want you to stay with me in the Holy of Holies no matter what your daily schedule may be" (Heb. 10:19–23).

What encouragement his words brought to my heart! "Lord, teach me; Holy Spirit, teach me; Father, teach me how to wait upon you all day. Teach me to take the backseat, to defer to you quickly and quietly, to deny my ego needs, and to be content to let you have full authority (Ps. 123:2)." I remembered Thomas Kelly, who so abided in Christ that the last three years of his life were spent in unbroken fellowship with the indwelling Holy Spirit. "They shall walk in the light of Thy countenance" (Ps. 89:15–16). Elton Trueblood knew Kelly in those years and said, "Thomas Kelly has been so much with Jesus that Jesus shines through him." How I yearned for that to be true of me—every moment bathed in his holy presence, my life exhibiting more and more of him and less and less of me! I longed to have his healing, loving presence flowing out in all he yearns to do through me.

It will surely take more than an hour a day to become like him. It will take clinging to the indwelling presence of Jesus all the time. Cleansing us from self-orientation will take him all the hours of every day of our lives! "The tragedy is that, though we are made for freedom, we are not really free, for we are bound by our own self-centeredness," writes Trueblood. "We put ourselves where we ought to put God."[14]

God's Commitment

One of the young women in our praying community had a growing desire to wait on God all day in her heart as she went about her work. Seated in a financial board meeting that was charged with stress and animosity, she felt her emotions begin to get the upper hand, her mind racing, her adrenaline pumping. Then she heard the Holy Spirit say, "Take a deep breath, come to me in your heart, relax."

She realized that to jump in and save the situation, as her fleshly instincts urged, would probably result in an ugly release of anger and resentment. Instead, she allowed the Holy Spirit to draw her into a deep interior quietness and listening to him about what she should do. As she sealed her outer lips, saying no to angry emotions within her, she began to experience his peace. "Lord," she began to pray, "let your presence come and flood this place. Come and take over this situation. Bring order and calm through me."

Suddenly a man on the board who seldom spoke said, "Let's all relax, take a deep breath, and calm ourselves. We can work this out."

The unspeakable peace of Jesus began to pull tempers and wills back onto a more rational plane, allowing space for people to get hold of themselves and turn from anger and impatience to quiet attitudes and harmony. What a joy to see him emerge strong in situations he can handle only as we remain reverent and lowly before him.

As we spend time daily with him, he will cause us to hunger and thirst for him far beyond some set time in the morning. We will long for the deepening companionship of intimate friendship all through the day. And continuous fellowship reveals what an unspeakable treasure he is. He causes us to love him so deeply that we would rather have his approval than the approval of others. Our need for validation from others begins to wane as his generous affirmation floods us. Our soul's sincere desire is to please him. The more we love him the more we are willing to take the lowly place. His presence begins to satisfy parts of us that have never been satisfied before.

He draws us into the reality that although we seem to be failing at every turn to remember him all through the day, he is still at work. He causes us to hate the times we are separated from him. We begin to see the stifling of Jesus' presence in us as the serious offense that it is. As we see the death that self produces when we yield to self-advantage and self-bias (Rom. 8:5–8), we begin to understand the enmity we display toward God when we do things our way, and we begin to draw back from displeasing God in this way. Our sins of judgment, criticism, lovelessness, and drawing attention to ourselves to prove we are significant begin to appear as black as they really are. Seeing how self-promoting we are causes us to cry out to the Holy Spirit, "Help me, save me from myself." He causes us to remember him (John 14:26) more throughout the day. Our workplaces, our modes of transportation, our homes are filled with more of him. Only the Holy Spirit can cause us to turn more readily to Jesus and find all of our pleasure in him.

Agnes Sanford says it well: "Only the Holy Ghost, the Sanctifier, can keep us in the love of Jesus and protect us from the anger and bitterness of this world and bring us into the glory of the Sons of God."[15]

Our Commitment

I hope this chapter has conveyed the truth that as necessary as our intentional, daily time of laying aside everything to wait on him is, our continuing to wait on him all through the day, literally moment by moment, is equally crucial.

As we move out of our quiet, tucked away places of waiting and enter into the tremendous external pressures of work and activity, it behooves us to ask the Holy Spirit to keep us steady and attentive to him. I believe he enjoys this challenge! We need to wait submissively on him in order to say no to self; this is difficult to achieve because we are so full of ourselves. The working out of our salvation involves this very staying with him in fear and trembling lest we rush out ahead of him in any way (Phil. 2:12).

We are so accustomed to operating out of our soulish realm with its self-stained personality, rebellious self-will, and self-promoting emotions. But as we wait we begin to discover how much there is of us in our daily living, and how little there is of him. As we begin to wait on God our behavior will change little at first, but as the weeks and months go by our love for him will increase. As that happens we will not want to miss him or forget him all day long; we will not want to be on our own. We will want him to teach us how to avoid the inner panic and stimulation that come from too much hurry and push; the "kicking in" of old emotional and mental patterns that produce nothing but anxiety and fear. We will long to be changed. As we cry out more and more in earnest, he will empower us to remember his presence within, even as our excited nervous and emotional systems start to take over. He will remind us that we have a choice: "Yield yourselves unto God . . . and your members as instruments of righteousness unto God" (Rom. 6:13). Make a choice, in other words, to go with God and his way of doing things. Relax, cry out to the Holy Spirit to help you calm down, to get your eyes back on Jesus. All of this can go on deep in your human spirit, even while chaos rules outside you. At the first urging of self and pride, allow your will to cry out for his strength and power.

As we have waited and been in his Word, we have been empowered by the Holy Spirit. But the choice is ours, "to be dead indeed unto sin, but alive unto God through Jesus Christ our Lord" (Rom. 6:11). Deep within our spirits we will begin to hear him speaking an encouraging word such as Ephesians 4:29–30: "Let no corrupt communication proceed out of your mouth, but that which is good to the use of edifying, that it may minister grace unto the hearers. And grieve not the Holy Spirit of God, whereby ye are sealed unto the day of redemption."

Sometimes, to speak an encouraging word is to speak correctively in love (Eph. 4:15). As we learn to wait on him throughout the day, we begin to see that the dear Holy Spirit will rise up within us, if we give him the smallest opportunity, he will cause us to speak encouragingly even to ourselves to refrain from grieving the Holy Spirit within us. We should not speak to anyone outside ourselves until we are under his control, until we have turned quickly to him for his words. Our passion becomes not to grieve the indwelling Spirit by failing to allow him to help us be obedient.

Often I quickly pray this way, "Jesus help me, empower me to say nothing to anyone until you have spoken peace to me, and in your grace, I speak to my troubled emotions and mind. I relax; I yield to you. There is plenty of time to do what needs to be done in and through you. I refuse to become agitated and lose your peace in my heart. I plead the blood of Jesus over my emotions, my mind, and my nervous system. I decree, as Job 22:28 says, 'Thou shalt also decree a thing, and it shall be established unto thee: and the light shall shine upon thy ways.' I decree your presence to be greater than this difficulty, and that your very life is being poured out over me and through me to others." A sincere prayer like this will bring situations under his control. Many times he only needs one person to be in touch with him to give him an opening to deal with the situation.

All the time I am silently praying this prayer of affirmation, positive and full of faith, I am relaxing, letting go to the Holy Spirit. Nothing is crossing my lips while I am positioning myself close to the cross and clinging to Jesus. All my soulish energies are being brought under the control of the indwelling Holy Spirit. My ego, which wants to rush in and "solve" the situation for self-reward, is pulled back under the Holy Spirit. I have spoken nothing audible out of the soulish realm, which would surely get me into trouble.

There are thousands of opportunities moment by moment down through each day to practice waiting and yielding to him. As we do, we find that he strengthens us "with might by his Spirit in the inner man" (Eph. 3:16), in remarkably quick and powerful ways.

In the very instance of need, literally on the spot with the storm raging all around us, without and within our soulish realm, the wondrous Holy Spirit helps us pull out of the emotional and mental storm produced by feeling overwhelmed and tempted. We run back under his shelter so he can be in control (Prov. 18:10). He wants us to draw on him moment by moment in unbroken fellowship. We cannot do any of the right things at such a time; all we can do is allow him to empower us to make the choice to stay with him, to wait on him to send his life flowing through us. We can do literally nothing until he gets us under control.

Our wills are strengthened with each episode. He empowers us so our wills become stronger in him and make the choice for him even though our flesh is stirred (John 15).

How easy it is to allow haste, caused by the pressure and anxiety in a tense situation, to trigger in us the urge to push out on our own. "I can handle it; get out of my way and let me show you!" In that rush, we simply forget him. It does not take much in a tense situation for pride and ego needs to want to take control. Remember, the forces of darkness want us to assume responsibility and allow the flesh to take over.

A hardworking husband returned home to find his wife, the mother of his three children, upset and angry over the day's events. His immediate inner reaction was, "Listen, I've been through unbelievable things myself today. Let me tell you about my day!"

But he had been waiting ten minutes on God each day in his forty-five minutes of daily quiet time, and the Holy Spirit had been urging him to continue in that humble, waiting mode all day. Down in his spirit he heard the Holy Spirit say, "Let my loving patience flow through you right now. In your impatience, turn to my fruit of the Spirit, patience, and listen to your wife."

The young husband took a deep breath, received the Holy Spirit's fruit of patience, and set aside himself and all he wanted to say. He put his arms around his wife and said, "Tell me all about it."

His obedience to the Holy Spirit and his ability to hear him speak, through humble practice, was rewarded. He found his heart flooded with God's love for his wife. The Holy Spirit's love turned a potential blowup into a tremendous blessing for both of them.

Once again let me emphasize the great spiritual law inherent in this discussion: *We will never be able to turn to him during the day unless we are allowing him time to take control of us as we wait on him with intentionality.* You will find, as I have, a shocking degree of failure to remember that we are still waiting before him, dependent and helpless, in the midst of heated situations. But the wonder of Jesus' power and love lies in the truth that he can take even our terrible failures and turn them into good if we walk humbly in obedience. If I fail and let temper and anger take over, I can, by his power only, go to the people involved and acknowledge my sin and failure, asking them to forgive me. As we repent and confess our own waywardness, he can share his life of love through us.

A Christian lawyer told me recently, "I had to humble myself before my client and ask his forgiveness. I had let pride take over in our transaction and was boastful and rude. The Holy Spirit would not let me rest until I had confessed that sin in the flesh."

The person of whom he asked forgiveness was so touched that he asked the lawyer about his devotional habits. The lawyer told him he was waiting on God, not just for twenty minutes of his devotional hour but all through the day. How wonderful that Jesus can redeem our failures and make them powerful tools for witness when we allow him to correct and humble us in public confession.

Medical science has said much in the last few years about the destructiveness of stress, which opens the door to illnesses of all kinds. As we stay close to him, waiting and listening throughout the day, we stay peaceful and calm, not upset or disturbed. Our health, both physical and emotional, can only be helped as we anchor ourselves in him, allowing faith and confidence in him to take over, rather than fear and anxiety.

We can live any way we want; this is still a free country. But what we give out we will get back, as Galatians 6:7 says: "Be not deceived; God is not mocked: for whatsoever a man soweth, that shall he also reap." How much better it is to give out, not from self-centered flesh but from his presence of love flowing through us to others. Psalm 112:7 says, "He shall not be afraid of evil tidings: his heart is fixed, trusting in the LORD." Verse 8 goes on to say, "His heart is established, he shall not be afraid." To live out of the indwelling Holy Spirit in our human spirit is the most thrilling of human experiences. To move out in sinful flesh is surely the saddest. He wants us to become fixed in him, not allowing any external circumstances to define our attitudes or our actions, or to limit our wonderful Lord in helping us and others with his life-giving love.

He continually draws us on to be present to him, waiting on him and for him, not only for a few minutes a day but continually (Hosea 12:6)!

Consequences of Cooperation with God

Life's experiences do humble us, but daily waiting can be our main source of humility.

Margaret Therkelsen

have opened previous chapters with personal illustrations of how God manifests his presence in our waiting. This chapter, however, can begin only with the greatest illustration of waiting—the one found in the Book of Acts. The presence of the Holy Spirit was so real, so manifest, the strong presence, the leader of all leaders for whom Peter, James, John, and all the others were awaiting in Jerusalem as Jesus had directed. His was the wisdom and knowledge of God, the manifest power of God, his was the Spirit of God and Spirit of Jesus. Everything they needed would be found in the Holy Spirit.

This was true not only of the apostles, who had seen Jesus with their eyes and handled him with their hands (1 John 1:1), but also of everyone in the gathering of 120 in the upper room. Prestige and experience meant nothing. The presence of the resurrected Jesus, the Holy Spirit, within them, was the crucial fact. His presence was more real and significant than who they were in the human realm. His presence literally overwhelmed them, yet it did not destroy their individuality.

The Holy Spirit had to be powerful within those early believers not only to bring forth the church of Jesus Christ but to establish and maintain it through supernatural power. They drew on him minute by minute. The Book of Acts relates one episode after another of waiting, praying, worshiping, and adoring wherein the Holy Spirit was granted supreme leadership and allowed to flourish as everything they needed!

Those who waited for the Holy Spirit obeyed him, doing whatever was necessary to maintain his heavenly supremacy. An initial ten days of humbling and cleansing from self-bias allowed them to become one in purpose. Waiting on God, helpless and powerless, taught them not to make a move until he came forth to guide them. Their abandonment to live solely by the life of God within was simple, yet profound.

The early disciples' behavior is still our pattern today. "Wait for the promise of the Father . . . ye shall be baptized with the Holy Ghost . . . ye shall receive power, after that the Holy Ghost is come upon you" (Acts 1:4–5, 8). We are not to wait occasionally, or only in times of crisis; we are to wait consistently day by day for the renewing of the Holy Spirit within us (Eph. 5:18).

The Holy Spirit was the "main act," not only for the 120 in the upper room but for the thousands who were added to the church. God himself was living in and through these followers, with results no mere human band could ever produce. All of human history was altered forever! Some results of their waiting, of allowing God to take over and build the church his way, are included in the following list.

1. Devout men out of every nation under heaven heard God speak to them in their own language (Acts 2:5–6). The Holy Spirit taught the truth about Jesus through Peter in authority and authenticity so that many believed (Acts 2:41).
2. The Holy Spirit opened listeners' ears to hear Peter preach; the Spirit also convicted them as they listened. The Holy Spirit enabled them to repent, to be baptized, and to receive the Holy Spirit into their hearts (Acts 2:41).
3. The disciples experienced steadfastness, consistency, as they let God turn their lives upside down. They literally lived only for him and in him (Acts 2:42). Their personal lives were secondary to letting God live his life within them.
4. So powerful was the Holy Spirit in manifestation that a holy reverence, a fear, was upon them. No one wanted to offend or trespass against the august presence of God in their midst (Acts 2:43). Submission to him and a godly fear resulted as the Holy Spirit did many wonders and signs, healing and redeeming through the believers. (We have little fear or awe in our church gatherings today; we talk, laugh, gossip, and fail to humble ourselves in the presence of the Lord. We need to enter our churches on Sunday morning and go at once into prayerful waiting on God, waiting for his presence to come. John Henry Jowett, a famous preacher of another day, has said, "We are not subdued into the receptiveness of awe.")[16]

5. The early believers literally abandoned themselves to the Holy Spirit, giving up possessions and goods so everyone could live in simplicity but in enough comfort to focus only and always on him (Acts 2:44–45).

6. Their allegiance to the Holy Spirit as their triumphant leader was so that they had harmony and oneness, giving themselves to the forms of spirituality that continually released them to his presence: prayer, waiting, worshiping, and the Lord's Supper (Acts 2:42, 46–47).

7. Within the fellowship of the early church each one knew his or her place in the body of Christ. Together they walked in oneness of heart and mind (Acts 4:32). This was truly a miracle because there was no competition between them; the Holy Spirit gave each of them place and dignity in his life.

8. They were a happy, joyful group, finding favor with God and all the people (Acts 2:42–47).

9. God brought in thousands of people to be a part of the church. As they waited and prayed, the Holy Spirit was allowed to do the kingdom work in their midst: He drew; he filled; he convicted; he trained; he did it all as they waited in sincere submission. He was the only one who could do God's work (Acts 2:32–33).

These results reveal the consequences of being under the control of the strong and loving leadership of the Holy Spirit. He was given authority to be the one in control of this vast group of men and women who moved only as he led, giving him supremacy. And he met all of their needs.

But a frightening depth of prideful need for self-glory and self-exultation is revealed in the story of Ananias and Sapphira (Acts 5). How disturbing to see that even in the holy atmosphere of the early church during those first months and years when the Holy Spirit was reigning within the believers so totally and powerfully, self still showed its ugly face. Ananias's and Sapphira's pride and stubborn selfishness tempted them to keep some of God's money for themselves. In sinning against the Holy Spirit, God himself, they were struck dead. The Holy Spirit's absolute authority had dealt with the offenders swiftly and publicly. Great fear came upon all the church and people outside the church (vv. 1–11). If in this period of church history we see the depth of sin and its power, we should marvel at where we are today. We seem to get away with everything, but God will deal with us and is dealing with us even as he dealt with the early church. "We have to do with the persistence of the self-life," wrote G. Campbell Morgan. "I often feel that the enemy I dread most is not the devil, not the problems by which I am surrounded, but myself. The reappearance of the self-life is perpetual. Immediately a man thinks he has gained a victory over it, mastered it, it garbs itself in other vestments and appears anew."[17]

The Book of Acts reveals the manifest victory and power available to us if we will sell out to the indwelling Holy Spirit as our ancestors did. The life of God lived in our midst produces enormous good. The Book of the Acts of the Holy Spirit (so named because it records the life of God the Holy Spirit flowing through the believers) tells us of the great harmony possible between the promise of the Father and the believer. Fruit is inevitable through this merger (John 15). He yearns for oneness with us even as he had with Jesus. But it will happen only with our permission (John 17:21).

I realize God gave the full measure of the Holy Spirit because his empowerment was necessary to birth the church of Jesus Christ and to establish it against great odds of brutality. Even though this historic event was a onetime experience, the pattern of waiting modeled by the early disciples is viable for us today. All the forces of hell led by Lucifer himself came against the early church. These forces continue, and only the life of the Holy Spirit in the believer can overcome the enemy's continuing onslaught. The fullest expression of the Holy Spirit within the believer is not an option but a necessity (Eph. 6:10–18).

Whatever was necessary to release the Holy Spirit then is necessary now to rekindle and renew the church in the same complete authority of his revealed, manifest presence. What would happen if Christians in all denominations would begin to wait on God both privately and corporately? What would happen if our pastors would call upon all Christians to enter the sanctuary and wait humbly on God? I believe our wonderful Lord would have the access he needs to come forth as our triumphant leader. We would see his power and his love pouring out from his people as in the days of Acts.

This book has focused on his interior life within the believer, drawing us into inner wholeness and holiness by the power of his manifest presence within. Only then can he flow through us, unhindered, out to others. As he gains control through our daily, increasing receptiveness and responsiveness to the Holy Spirit, he is granted more and more dominion within us and more availability to flow through us. The thrust of the original Pentecost is over, but we must live lives of yieldedness that begin in our private time with God as we wait on him. Then our corporate church life will reflect the power of the Holy Spirit.

In this final chapter it would be impossible to share all the consequences that come as we set aside ourselves and wait for him to manifest his presence. What God does is so lavish, so generous beside our paltry attempts, that we marvel at the depth of his love for us. The struggle to lay self aside can be bitter, but he honors any attempt at all in amazing ways. These early believers knew the devastation of their human limitations so thoroughly; they understood that only God could produce the needed goal. They saw the consequences of disobedience to the Holy Spirit and lived in humble, lowly obedience.

We have wandered so far afield of his august, manifest presence, taking matters into our own hands. As a result we have seen little fruit and do not even believe he can be Lord over us, and in us, all we need. The blunt truth is we feel we must run our own lives because he cannot be trusted to do it. Zechariah 4:6 says, "Not by might, nor by power, but by my spirit, saith the LORD of hosts." Our foolishness in trusting ourselves to bring about what only God can do reflects the self-determination and self-exaltation of our age.

The pure Holy Spirit can manifest himself far beyond our sensual, sexual, soulish realm so unmistakably that everyone recognizes the holy, selfless, clear-cut presence of Jesus in our midst. But this kind of manifestation comes only as we allow the Holy Spirit to empty us of everything that smacks of self-orientation.

The only biblical pattern is that of waiting upon him, allowing the Holy Spirit to reveal himself, both privately and corporately, and letting him reveal to us the awful limitations of the flesh. Following this pattern drives us deeper into his life within us.

The Holy Spirit has convicted me as I have prayerfully sought to allow him to flow through me in this book. I yearn beyond any ability to describe to yield more and more of myself to him, so he is increased and I am decreased! When we cooperate with him he cooperates with us (James 4:8).

The Results of Cooperation

When God's commitment and my commitment come together we see amazing results. As we reflect on what God wants to do in our lives, we become keenly aware that God is not a respecter of persons but of the conditions in our life. Basic to this understanding is that as I come into his presence with intentionality and openness, he will manifest himself to me. There is no way to articulate the outcome of waiting on God. It is beyond the scope of human understanding and is personalized to meet our uniqueness to the extent that we open ourselves. As a point of departure for your journey of waiting on God, let me offer a few of the marvelous consolations of his presence.

1. We learn the joy of surrender. As we wait on God and begin to discover the promise of the Father, we gain new insights into the meaning of the word *surrender.* Our old narrow understanding of a onetime surrender is replaced with a newer understanding that goes far beyond anything we have ever experienced. It is like the child who has always known something of what it means to study but is now captivated by a particular subject and cannot wait to explore it to the fullest.

As we begin the surrender process, we become aware of the power that is available to us. We have never experienced this before, or if we have, it has been in a much more limited way. The surrender process involves handing over more of ourselves—our opinions, our desires, our "pet" ideas, our stubbornness, and our rebellion. This process is much like immersing an object in a tub of water: The more the object is submerged in the water, the more the water spills over the side of the tub. As we submerge more and more of ourselves in the life of the Holy Spirit, more of the Holy Spirit spills out onto the world around us. The believers we read about in the Book of Acts experienced this very thing. They had no other source of power than to submerge themselves in the presence of the Holy Spirit, waiting on him, ministering to him even as Acts 13:1–4 explains. No one else could help them in the face of persecution and death. Only his power could perform his will. They also knew they would not experience his power unless they acted in his way, in his time. They did not want to get in his way and were willing to lay down everything for his presence to be made manifest. They experienced ever-deepening levels of surrender because they had no other choice. The inevitable result of yieldedness was then, and is now, his strong presence that restrains us from acting out of human strength (Acts 7:54–60).

2. We please him with our friendship. The prophet Isaiah tells us how much God wants us to be his friends and that as we wait, he will come to meet us. "And therefore will the LORD wait, that he may be gracious unto you, and therefore will he be exalted, that he may have mercy upon you: . . . blessed are all they that wait for him" (Isa. 30:18). In Genesis 3:8–9 we learn how God came to the garden to be with Adam and Eve. He even called out to Adam, demonstrating how much he sought their companionship, and seeks ours, as well. "And they heard the voice of the LORD God walking in the garden in the cool of the day: . . . And the LORD God called unto Adam, and said unto him, Where art thou?"

Our waiting on God touches him profoundly. It is a demonstration of humility and utter dependence on him, which is, of course, the only right way to relate to him. It is the breaking open of our lives, our devotion, and our love being poured out to bless him. Waiting on God is truly an alabaster box of love that costs us something; it is a sweet-smelling perfume in his nostrils (John 12:1–8).

God fully understands our sacrifices of time, attention, and praise. He knows waiting is far harder for us to do than ministry and service projects. Waiting is simply "being there" for him because we love him. One reason waiting is such a struggle is that we do it in secret; our egos, therefore, do not get the strokes that we get from others when we engage in public ministry.

Waiting is the beginning stage of learning to abide or live with God. There are appropriate ways to come into the presence of God that are pleasing to him. Out of my own personal experience I have found that to come into his presence and allow him to unfold who he is within me seems to please him immensely. Often I will come with my Scriptures open on my lap and open my heart to him and his Word. He is a living person who desires friendship! We ponder his words and he begins to teach us how to live with him: "Abide in me, and I in you. As the branch cannot bear fruit of itself, except it abide in the vine; no more can ye, except ye abide in me" (John 15:4). Since waiting develops friendship with God, we develop a great yearning to live in the state of harmony of which John chapter 15 speaks. We want to become more like him, so his nature empowers our will to do what is right more continuously.

God wants to be with us, even more than we want to be with him. He is waiting for us; he yearns to be to us all we need (Song of Sol. 2:8–14).

Only those who experience the unspeakable reality of the Holy Spirit as he pushes back the clouds from Jesus, so we see him more and more as he is and grows the transforming life of God within us, can begin to believe that God truly desires intimacy with us (Gal. 4:19). The condition of our fallen nature, with its terrible defacing of self-worth through the awfulness of sin, causes us to doubt he cares for each one of us, because we have not experienced his powerful love. But as we wait before him (Micah 7:7), quietly placing ourselves before his throne of grace and giving ample time to the waiting whether we feel he shows up or not, he reveals his tender and loving self (Isa. 30:18). He yearns for us to come; he calls out to us, speaking our names. He wants to be with us. All is ready. He has done all he can do. Will you come? (See Lam. 3:25–26.)

3. We enter a whole new realm of caring for him. His presence breaking in upon us more and more causes us to love him in growing consecration and depth. We enter a whole new realm of caring for him. We feel deeper love coming to us from the Father, Son, and Holy Spirit. Experiences with each member of the Trinity come more and more into focus.

We can never fully know the sacredness of God's life, his worth and value, but we can see in a more penetrating way the intensity of his love not only for us but for everyone. We enter what the saints call "bridal love," the heartfelt, adoring love that a bride has for her bridegroom. His love in us causes us to love him in return. And we want him to love through us with divine love (Matt. 25:1–13; 1 John 4:20–21).

Our love for God becomes so life changing that we willingly face our inner disorder and sin, asking him to cleanse us so we are more like him. Waiting on God allows one of the most miraculous things to happen: He enables our wills to obey him more and more. Without waiting on God we simply cannot do in our own strength what we know we should. His love alters us, giving us love to obey and faith to trust (Gal. 5:6).

4. We trust him more and more. Faith begins to rise up in us. Faith operates by love as we trust him more and more. He teaches us that the soulish realm, the realm of our five senses, cannot be trusted. We are not to live out of that realm but rather through dependence on the Holy Spirit within our human spirit. He wants us to relate to the Holy Spirit on an entirely new plane of consciousness, not out of personality or willpower; instead, we receive his divine nature (2 Peter 1:3–4) in such a way that he comes forth through us! We lean less on feelings and our mental state, and more on him.

The Holy Spirit will begin to deal with our impatience, which is one of the greatest hindrances to spiritual growth. It flows out of self-love, which feels things should go our way. We love our own way more than God's way, or we would not become so upset when things go differently than what we think is best.

He wants to bring us into rest and peace, which keep us patient and calm enough to be able to hear him speak (Luke 21:19). He longs to converse with us.

The waiting becomes resting, as we sink down into his peace, so our needs do not seem larger than he is (John 14:27)! We know when we have lost the peace; we are outside him and in the soulish realm. We hurry to him for that peace, that rest, to be restored (James 3:17–18; Eph. 2:14).

5. We experience his "tailor-made" teaching. Only the Holy Spirit can teach us how to wait, because each one of us is unique. James 4:5 says, "The Spirit that dwelleth in us lusteth to envy." This means that he jealously wants to interact with the deepest part of ourselves and with our shallowest parts too. As I wait day by day, I find myself less afraid of him, and he teaches me how to receive him.

He causes me to face my sin nature, my woundedness, to let him help me as he cleanses my inner nature by the power of the blood of Jesus. As the daily cleansing continues, I find myself emerging in him as the person he made me to be; I experience my real personhood in and through him. The wonder is that I have failed to appropriate him as my heart yearned to. Yet he accepts me as I am! What joy and what peace! The more I relate to him, the more my new personhood comes forth, and he helps me relate to others and myself through the ministry of the Holy Spirit.

6. We learn new ways to worship him. Waiting brings us into true worship of God, Jesus, and the Holy Spirit. I love Evelyn Underhill's definition of pure worship: "It asks for nothing, it does not want to improve anything, it is not concerned for what religion does for us, with 'profit of godliness'. It is content to adore God, to worship Him, in self-forgetfulness."[18]

As we wait on him to be the initiator, we enter a richer, larger universe where we see him as he is. Our problems, when seen from God's perspective, can be laid aside as we worship in the Holy Spirit within our spirit, and in the truth as he sees the truth!

The Holy Spirit will manifest his gifts and the fruits of our abiding as we worship him. The wondrous anointing of the Holy Spirit, the quintessence of Jesus' nature, his love, and his power, will well up within us and flow out to others in prayer and as we walk out our lives each day. In a deep sense we will stand aside as he comes forth through us, and we will know beyond any doubt that Jesus is preeminent, not us.

As we become more emptied of self, his anointing will be released more often and with greater sweetness because we are out of the way. Nothing is more exciting than to yield to him as he empowers us to let him come forth (1 John 2:27).

7. *We yearn to be like Jesus.* As we wait on God our hearts yearn to be more like Jesus. We discover that we would rather be pure in heart than to have all public acclaim and fame. Each step of the waiting journey will unfold in a deepening passion to be like him at any cost.

Our many failures to be like him will cleanse us of pride, and we will weep with despair. Often, no one else will know of these inner battles, but he will know, and in our failures we will come to understand that we will never be like him by our own hand. To overcome ourselves is a gift from God the Holy Spirit, to whom we will cling more and more as our only hope for Christlikeness. Any character change at all will occur because he has been faithful to do all for us, in spite of us. Grace all the way and nothing but grace will fulfill our yearning to be like him!

Time with God is life changing. As the weeks and years pass, the ongoingness of his life in us will be utterly amazing. The process of waiting, whether through pondering Scripture or in quiet gazing upon him, will push back horizons of spiritual understanding we will only intuit through the Holy Spirit. He will continually cause us to drink the wine of astonishment (Ps. 60:3). "The path of the just is as the shining light, that shineth more and more unto the perfect day" says Proverbs 4:18. This life with him fulfills every sincere desire he has given us and reaches out into other lives in ways we could never imagine.

The life of God takes us from glory to glory (2 Cor. 3:18), and he is generous beyond expression. Waiting on him opens us up to him and all he is. As Andrew Murray put it, "The Holy Spirit is the real, living Presence and the power of the Father working in us."[19]

God's purpose in establishing the lordship of Jesus in our spirits through the Holy Spirit is that our bodies, souls, and spirits will be set aside for him. His "keeping power" is available to us, so our "whole spirit and soul and body will be preserved blameless unto the coming of our Lord Jesus Christ. Faithful is he that calleth you, who also will do it" (1 Thess. 5:23–24). This "keeping power" does not reside in the arm of flesh (Jer. 17:5–8). It resides only in our great High Priest, Jesus the holy and endless one. Our waiting allows him time and place to perform his high and holy office as we kneel before the mercy seat, his throne of grace (Isa. 25:9).

In the days to come only those who open their windows toward "Jerusalem" and face their God through Scripture and quiet waiting will be able to stand (Dan. 6:10).

It is my earnest prayer that you will deem him worthy of all praise, of all waiting, and that you will let him fill you over and over with himself, so he can triumph in and through you. Nothing is too difficult for him (Jer. 32:17–27).

Notes

1. Andrew Murray, *The Holiest of All: An Exposition of the Epistle to the Hebrews* (Grand Rapids: Revell, 1993), 30.

2. A. W. Tozer, *The Pursuit of God* (Camp Hill, Penn.: Christian Publications, 1993), 40–42.

3. Quotes of Starr Daily in chapter 3 are from his sharing of his testimony, which I was privileged to hear on numerous occasions.

4. Thomas Dubay, S.M., *Fire Within* (San Francisco: Ignatius Press, 1989), 113.

5. Charles Spurgeon, "The Barrier," in *Classic Sermons on Heaven and Hell,* comp. Warren W. Wiersbe (Grand Rapids: Kregel, 1994), 123.

6. Andrew Murray, *Waiting on God* (Pittsburgh: Whitaker House, 1981), 25.

7. Oswald Chambers, *Still Higher for His Highest* (Grand Rapids: Zondervan, 1970), 58.

8. Watchman Nee, *Introduction of Spirit, Soul, Body,* vol. 1 (New York: Christian Fellowship Publishers, 1977), 193.

9. Jessie Penn-Lewis, *Soul and Spirit* (Poole, England: The Overcomer Literature Trust, n.d.), 33.

10. Spurgeon, *Classic Sermons,* 121.

11. Watchman Nee, *The Spiritual Man* (New York: Christian Fellowship Publishers, 1977), 185–86.

12. Dubay, *Fire Within,* 113.

13. Murray, *Waiting,* 25.

14. Elton Trueblood, *The Lord's Prayer* (New York: Harper and Row, 1965), 52.

15. Agnes Sanford, *Sealed Orders* (Plainfield, N.J.: Logos International, 1972), 42.

16. Arthur Poritt, *John Henry Jowett* (New York: George Doran Co., 1925), 119.

17. G. Campbell Morgan, "The Strength of the Name," in *Classic Sermons on the Names of God,* comp. Warren W. Wiersbe (Grand Rapids: Kregel, 1993), 133.

18. Evelyn Underhill, *Life As Prayer* (Harrisburg, Penn.: Morehouse Publishing, 1946), 201.

19. Murray, *Waiting,* 24.

Margaret Therkelsen, a professional musician for over thirty-three years, was guided to become a counselor and retreat speaker on prayer and spiritual life. She received her master's degree in marriage and family therapy and has a successful counseling practice. She and her husband live in Lexington, Kentucky.